"Austin is an outstanding young man! He inspires us to dream bigger, reach higher, and love deeper. His story deserves a wide hearing."

—Max Lucado,
Author and Minister of Writing and
Preaching at Oak Hills Church

Austin Gutwein inspires me and makes me want to believe God for miracles! His life demonstrates the truth that God uses ordinary people to do His extraordinary work. I'm proud to call him my friend.

—Kay Warren,
Executive Director HIV/AIDS Initiative
Saddleback Church

"I am very impressed with Austin Gutwein's story in *Take Your Best Shot*. This book is filled with words of encouragement, inspiration, and hope. It's guaranteed to motivate you into action."

—Pat Williams,
Senior Vice President
Orlando Magic

"When people ask me how they can possibly make a difference fighting a problem as big as 'global poverty,' I tell them about a boy named Austin who, like David, stared Goliath in the eye without flinching. This young man has done more to make a difference in the lives of children orphaned by AIDS than most American churches, let alo~

If you are older than 10 and you haven't yet done your part to change the world, read *Take Your Best Shot* and be inspired. Austin Gutwein shows us the way."

—Richard Stearns, President, World Vision US,
Author of *The Hole in Our Gospel*

"I spent a day with Austin and his family and found them inspiring. His story, I believe, challenges us all. The first thing I thought as I drove to the airport was, *What was I doing when I was twelve?* And then, of course, the next thought: *What, exactly, am I doing now?*"

—John Larson,
Former NBC National Correspondent

"Every time I'm with this young man I want to say to him, *'Okay, Austin . . . let's you and I go out and conquer the world for Christ.'* That's the way he makes me feel. His ideas and dreams are already changing the face of an African nation . . . and he's only fifteen, for goodness' sake! With focused vision and dedication of heart, the encouragement of his parents, and the Spirit of God, Austin Gutwein is a 'one-kid-army' of hope. I love this guy. And I love his book. It's an absolute joy to read. Check it out for yourself."

—Luci Swindoll,
Speaker and Author with Women of Faith

"When people ask who has most impacted me over the last year, without hesitation I can say Austin Gutwein and the story of Hoops of Hope. I am around amazing leaders all the time, and Austin rivals all of them. Austin is my friend. And Austin is one of my heroes. At fifteen he has had more impact than most of us will ever have in our entire lives. I love the work of Hoops of Hope. You can't be around Austin, or the amazing work of Hoops of Hope, without being deeply impacted and inspired. Trust me. Do yourself a favor and read this book and the incredible story. But once you do, be prepared to be changed and challenged. You'll see the world and your significant role in helping those less fortunate in an amazingly fresh way."

—Brad Lomenick,
Executive Director, Catalyst

"Austin's story is one of modern-day heroism. He represents a new generation that can carry us all into the twenty-first century . . . a world of hope, peace, and selfless love. Austin completely inspires me."

—Daniel Biro,
Hawk Nelson

"We commend Austin for his example and testimony. His heart for orphans and desire to move his generation to action are an inspiration. We can't wait to see how God will use him and his message as he continues to 'do hard things' for him."

—Alex and Brett Harris,
Authors of *Do Hard Things: A Teenage Rebellion Against Low Expectations*

"All of us have met someone who truly inspires us; few of us have met someone who does so as young as Austin Gutwein. This young man and his story are simply remarkable. On his way to changing the world, he has changed our church, and he has changed me. Get ready to see what happens when youthfulness and creativity intersects vision and passion."

—Cal Jernigan,
Senior Pastor
Central Christian Church of the East Valley
Mesa, AZ

"Austin Gutwein is living proof that teenagers aren't the church of tomorrow; they are the church of today! I have been a youth pastor for over twenty years, and the entire time I have been telling students that God is in the business of using young people to make a difference. In this book, Austin shares his incredible story and shows us an example of what God can do through teenagers who are willing to take their best shot."

—Kurt Johnston,
Pastor to Students
Saddleback Church

take
Your Best
SHOT

do something bigger than yourself

By **Austin Gutwein**

with Todd Hillard

THOMAS NELSON
Since 1798

NASHVILLE   DALLAS   MEXICO CITY   RIO DE JANEIRO

Published in Nashville, Tennessee, by Thomas Nelson. Thomas Nelson is a registered trademark of Thomas Nelson, Inc.

Published in association with the literary agency of Alive Communications, Inc., 7680 Goddard Street, Suite 200, Colorado Springs, CO 80920. www.alivecommunications.com.

Photos © 2008–2009 Dan Gutwein. Maggie photo © 2008 Jon Warren/World Vision.

Thomas Nelson, Inc., titles may be purchased in bulk for educational, business, fund-raising, or sales promotional use. For information, please e-mail SpecialMarkets@ThomasNelson.com.

Unless otherwise noted, Scripture quotations are taken from the *Holy Bible*, New Living Translation. © 1996, 2004. Used by permission of Tyndale House Publishers, Inc., Wheaton, Illinois 60189. All rights reserved.

Scripture quotations marked NIV are from the HOLY BIBLE: NEW INTERNATIONAL VERSION®. © 1973, 1978, 1984 by International Bible Society. Used by permission of Zondervan Publishing House. All rights reserved.

Library of Congress Cataloging-in-Publication Data

Gutwein, Austin.
 Take your best shot : do something bigger than yourself / by Austin Gutwein, with Todd Hillard.
    p. cm.
 Includes bibliographical references.
 ISBN 978-1-4003-1515-4 (pbk.)
 1. Church work with the sick. 2. AIDS (Disease)—Religious aspects—Christianity. 3. Church work. 4. Christian life. 5. Gutwein, Austin. I. Hillard, Todd, 1963– II. Title.
 BV4460.7.G88 2009
 261.8'321969792—dc22   2009018708

Printed in the United States of America

10 11 12 13 RRD 8 7 6 5

Mfg. by RRD
Crawfordsville, Indiana
March 2010
PPO #104868

This book is dedicated to my sister Brittany.

Thank you for always being there behind the scenes.

Thank you for your encouragement.

Thank you for always knowing how to make me laugh.

I love you.

You are my hero and my best friend.

Contents

The Beauty of an Assist

By Luke Ridnour

When I was a kid, I was what you might call a "gym rat." My father was a basketball coach, and we shared a passion for the game. In fact, I became so obsessed with basketball that by the time I was a sophomore in high school, I had my own set of keys to the gym. Over the years, I have learned there are many parallels to the game of basketball and to walking with God. One of which I see clearly spelled out in what Hoops of Hope and Austin Gutwein are trying to accomplish.

It's called an assist.

An *assist* is when one player passes the ball to another so the team can score. It is not just about passing the ball, but passing it in the right way, at the right time. You may not know it, but passing the ball is one of the most desired skills in a basketball player. Had I not learned this skill, I would never have made it through high school and college basketball and into the NBA. A *selfish* player is only thinking about himself and for his opportunity to score. The truth is, selfish players rarely make it in the NBA. On the other hand, a *self-less* player is looking for all opportunities on the court. It's not just about him. His eyes are open at all times. He has an awareness of where everyone is, even if he is not looking in their direction.

NBA players like John Stockton and "Pistol" Pete Maravich were masters of the assist. Just watching them inspired me to play better. Their teammates loved them for their ability to pass, and, as a result, they won many games and championships.

Now, I want to introduce you to the masters of a new kind of assist: Austin Gutwein and Hoops of Hope. Austin could be just like any other teenager, playing video games and hanging out with his friends. Instead, he, and many other kids like him around the country, are putting together these free-throw shooting events to raise money for HIV/AIDS orphans in Africa, and in the process, offering a huge assist. Once again, I am inspired.

So let me ask you: Are your eyes on yourself, or are you aware of what is happening to others? Is it all about you? Or have you made yourself a part of a team? Don't get me wrong, I know how hard it can be to just live in this world, let alone try to help someone else. However, I firmly believe that if you will take the first steps to help others—God will meet you and *give you an assist*.

You see, I discovered a long time ago that with God all things are possible. *Take Your Best Shot* is not only the inspiring story of what a kid can do with a basketball, but what God can do through a kid.

—LUKE RIDNOUR, Milwaukee Bucks, NBA

Introduction

In 2004, nine-year-old Austin Gutwein set out on an unexpected journey that would touch the lives of children halfway around the world. It began with one small boy shooting free throws on a basketball court in Arizona. It became the internationally recognized organization Hoops of Hope. Today, thousands of kids and adults join Austin on World AIDS Awareness Day and throughout the year to raise money for orphans in Zambia, Africa. With over five hundred Hoops of Hope events held in seventeen countries, over one million dollars has been raised to help these children.

A story like Austin's comes around once in a blue moon, and it is a story best told in his own, very special voice. . . .

It all started with a very simple phrase:

"God wants to use you."

I can't tell you how many times I've heard that phrase. My parents have said that to me a thousand times. My Sunday school teachers and youth pastors seem to fit it into just about every lesson I've ever listened to. Seriously, if I only had a dollar for every time I've heard somebody say, "Austin, God wants to use you. . . ."

You know what, though? It is true. God does want to use you. He has used me, and I'm no different than you. I'm just a normal kid. You probably know lots of kids just like me—you know, the one who lives down the street, the guy with a sister and a dog (the guy who wonders why his sister never has to clean up after the dog), the guy who sits next to you in algebra class wondering if he's ever going to use this stuff in the real world.

I'm normal enough, but for some reason I've gotten swept along on an adventure that's totally *ab*normal. I never planned on it, and I never asked for it, but today I'm part of an amazing adventure that has taken me to four different continents, connected me to tens of thousands of incredible people, generated more than a million dollars (so far), and has caused me to miss endless days of school in the last two years alone. (I'll bet *that* got your attention!) And I don't even have a driver's license yet. Honestly, I don't even know how it's all happened. All I know is that I'm a normal kid who heard, "Austin, God wants to use you" enough times that I started to believe it.

I want you to believe it too. When you put your all into something, when you're so inspired or dedicated that you give it all you've got, you are **taking your best shot**. The goal can be big or small because the score doesn't matter. Taking your best shot is about letting God use you, and giving him your "A-game," to do something bigger than yourself.

Your adventure may not look exactly like mine, but trust me: it will be an adventure like no other. Here's something else that's awesome: as you read and begin to discover your own journey, you'll find out quickly that *you're not alone.*

Something is happening with our generation. Kids are really trying to make a difference in the world. They're reaching out to people in need, and they're stepping out of their comfort zones. Something is happening in their hearts. They want to take their best shot at this life; they want to do something bigger than themselves. Most of them aren't making a big deal about it. They are working behind the scenes. They come from all walks of life and see a lot of things differently, but there are a few things that almost everyone agrees on:

1. We are inheriting a world in great need. It seems like everywhere you look there is pain, poverty, and hopelessness. Soon enough all these problems will be our responsibility because we kids will grow up to be the pastors, the parents, the professionals, and the presidents of tomorrow.

2. The world expects so little out of us right now, it's almost ridiculous. Really, the best they hope for is that we don't get into too much trouble before we are old enough to vote. If we don't do drugs, don't drop out of school, don't have sex, and don't get arrested, that's success. That's crazy! Who set the bar so low for teenagers? Note to grown-ups: I know we are hard to figure out and we drive you crazy. I know we confuse you with our text-messaging ways. I know you wish we would pull our pants up above our belly buttons like you do. But please—expect more from us. We just might surprise you.

3. We believe we can make a difference at any age—no matter what our skills are, no matter what race or neighborhood we come from, no matter where we are in life. We can be used. It's time to make a difference in the world, *now*.

Teenagers are learning to unleash their personal passions in order to love God and love others in a powerful way, right where they are. They are doing things that might seem small, but they are things that truly matter. People are making a big difference, and it's all for things that really count.

You might not be there yet. You might still be searching for something to fill that empty space in your heart. You might still be looking around and wondering what life is truly all about. You might still be living for yourself and are just now starting to realize that you need something bigger than yourself to make life worthwhile. So if you're still searching, welcome to the journey! But I'm warning you to be careful. As you begin to see how God is using people around the world and how he wants to use you, you just might be changed forever.

The world is in great need, and something has to be

done. So ask yourself two important questions: Do I want to be a part of the solution? And am I ready to take my best shot? (If you can't answer "yes" to those questions right now, that's okay; keep reading.) We know that *we* are the ones who can and should be doing something bigger than ourselves, and we know that these things can and should be done *now*. But that still leaves one bigger question: How? How do we do this?

This is why I want to share my story. There's a pattern that I've seen in my own life and in the lives of those around me who are becoming world-changers. The group grows every time someone decides to help another person, but it doesn't start outside. It starts *inside*. Inside the heart, inside the mind, inside the soul. It's an inner journey that changes the outward life. I think the journey looks like this:

We realize the world actually does *not* revolve around us.

We realize that we only have one life to live, only one chance to make it count.

We start off by focusing on who we *are* rather than what we *do*.

We discover that doing something bigger than ourselves begins with Someone bigger than ourselves.

We do a major motivation check.

We embrace our own passions and adopt our own purposes.

We are willing to dream big and act small.

We partner with others who are going in similar directions.

We prepare for desertion, opposition, and distraction.

We celebrate like crazy when cool things happen around us.

We willingly join this group of people who are taking their best shot and doing things that are bigger than themselves.

Just so you know, that's the journey we are going to take together in this book. Along the way I will also share with you stories from the amazing continent of

Africa and the cool story of Hoops of Hope. You'll hear some pretty amazing stories from other people as well. But please understand something right away—Hoops of Hope is not about me. Hoops of Hope is something God has started in our generation. And this book is really about *your* story and how God wants to use *you* to touch people.

At school you might get in trouble for writing in your textbooks, but *Take Your Best Shot* is different. It's yours; it's your story. If you want to, get out some pens and mark it up. Circle stuff; underline things; draw all over it. There's even space to write at the end of each chapter. When you are done, you will have a personal, customized version of the story of God's change in *your* life.

Who would have ever dreamed that one kid, one video, a basketball, and a hoop in America could be used to change lives half a world away? Not me.

Yes, God wants to use you, and he's ready to use you *now*. Life is short, and the world is waiting. It's time to do something bigger than yourself. It's time to take your best shot.

chapter 1

Maggie

"God is in the slums, in the cardboard boxes
where the poor play house. God is in the
silence of a mother who has infected her child
with a virus that will end both their lives. God is
in the cries heard under the rubble of war. God
is in the debris of wasted opportunity and lives,
and God is with us if we are with them."

{ bono, lead singer of u2 }

I couldn't stop staring at the TV screen. The story was really scaring me, and the little girl . . . it was awful. She was in a place that was completely foreign to me. I had never seen anything like it. The landscape was beautiful, but everything else just seemed horrible. My dad had just put a DVD into the player. It was only four minutes long, but they were four minutes of the most powerful images I had ever seen, and it was the most powerful story I had ever heard. Pictures of the little girl and her life flooded our family room, like Africa was pulled right into our house through the television. I could see it. I could almost touch it. I could definitely feel it. Minute by minute, my life was being changed forever.

The little girl's name was Maggie. She and I were both nine years old when we met through the TV screen, but she had already experienced a lifetime of tragedy. She lived in Zambia, and she had lost the most important people in her life—her mother, her father, her aunts and uncles, her grandparents . . . even her little brother. They had all died of AIDS.

3

For the past few decades, this terrible disease has plagued Africa. The Human Immunodeficiency Virus (HIV) is a virus that hurts the immune system. When it gets really bad, it's called Acquired Immune Deficiency Syndrome (AIDS). Having AIDS means that illnesses or infections that your body would normally beat in a couple of days will end up killing you because your immune system has forgotten how to fight them. The virus is highly contagious, and passes from one person to another through sexual intercourse or exchange of blood (like through open cuts or sharing needles). The virus does not discriminate between different kinds of people; anyone can contract it, and there is a 15–30 percent chance that an infected pregnant mother will pass it to her baby. There are lots of drugs we have now that can help people with HIV and AIDS live longer, but there is no cure. AIDS is always fatal.

That's the reason Maggie was alone in the world. She lived in a mud hut just slightly bigger than a walk-in closet with her seventy-three-year-old great-grandmother; the only living relative she had left—and she was lucky. Most of the AIDS orphans in Africa have no one to care for them; they have no one at all. Maggie was also blessed that she didn't have HIV or AIDS herself.

She was going to live. But what kind of life would she have? She had no school, she had no bed, and she and her great-grandmother huddled under an old tarp when it rained because the water poured into their hut and made mud puddles on the floor. Each day Maggie and her great-grandmother woke up, not knowing if they would have food. Each day they tried to help their neighbors with gardening or cleaning up the village, hoping to earn something to eat. But some days they went without any food at all. Maggie stared at me. I stared at her. My heart was breaking for her, and then I realized: *If this could happen to her, it could happen to me.*

The narrator on the DVD said these words:

Maggie doesn't expect us to change the world. But you can help change hers. You have the power to impact the lives of one child. Unless you do nothing.[1]

Maggie Moments

Life around our house was pretty normal before Maggie came into our lives. When I was eight, our pastor, Rick Warren, preached a message called "Blessed to Be a

Blessing." An organization called World Vision was at our church that day, and after the service there were tables set up where people could pick up packets to sponsor a child from really poor parts of the world. We found out $35 a month would supply a child with food, clothing, and an education. My parents brought me and my sister to the tables and told us we could each pick one. I picked out a little boy named Ignatius from Uganda, Africa. I wanted to find out about where he lived, so I started learning about Africa. It was the first time I realized that not everyone lives like I live here in the United States. It really caught my attention, particularly when Ignatius and I started writing letters back and forth. It was cool, and it was interesting, but for the most part, life around the Gutwein house didn't really change.

Then we got the videos. A year later World Vision sent us a sponsor packet that had *Maggie's Story* in it. As I watched, I just kept thinking about what it would be like if *I* lost *my* parents. It was hard to actually imagine. It was hard for my brain to get a picture of what that would be like. What if I didn't have a house to go home to? What if I didn't even have a bed to climb into each night? What if I were alone? What if I were the one who was trying to sleep under the tarp when the rains poured through the thin grass of my roof? *What if I were Maggie?* Maggie didn't ask for that life. She had no more control over it than I did. I just happened to be born in America, while she was born in Zambia. Why was she there? And why was I here? All the questions pointed to the one question that turned my life upside down. I finally asked myself, *What if this were me?*

In that moment some sort of connection was made between my heart and my brain. I call it a "Maggie Moment." It's a little hard to explain, but it was like everything suddenly became real—me, my family,

In the spring of 2009, I was able to travel to Uganda to meet Ignatius and his family. It was an awesome experience! Here we are going to get water from the well.

Africa . . . life. I started to see the world for what it is, and I started to discover my place in it. It was kind of like I woke up, or maybe I just grew up, right there watching the TV. I don't know. All I know is that I started to think. And I started to think differently. Everything around me looked the same, and yet somewhere *inside* me everything had changed. I was able to get outside of myself for the first time. There was more to life than just my little world. Somewhere, on the other side of the globe, Maggie was out there. She could have been huddled under a tarp with her great-grandmother on a mud floor at that very moment. My heart was broken, and I decided to do something about it.

My Maggie Moment came through a video. For others, it might come through an illness, the death of someone you love, or getting lied to by a friend. Your Maggie Moment might come from something you read in the Bible or some other experience entirely. Whatever it is, God takes Maggie Moments and uses them to flip on a switch in our hearts and in our brains . . . and it changes everything. Maggie Moments can be big, or they can be small, but they change us forever. They wake us up, and they tell us that there is a new kind of life waiting for us. They make us ask difficult questions and cause us to face painful realities. Maggie Moments can inspire us to do something bigger than ourselves and take our best shot to help people who don't deserve to be poor any more than I deserved to not be poor.

I don't know if you've ever experienced a Maggie Moment, and I'm not sure what it's going to look like when you do. In fact, I don't know if you've experienced anything like what I just described. All I know is that it's a huge world out there, filled with billions of people who are all Maggies in their own way. Some are lonely. Some are struggling to find God. Some are sick, and some are hungry. Some people need clean water, and some people just need a friend. There may be an elderly lady down your street who needs her lawn mowed, or a lonely kid in your class who needs someone to sit with at lunch. Stop and think for a moment. Can you see a face in need?

Most people think world-changers need to be strong, smart, and popular. Most people also think you need to be a certain age. I don't think so. I think becoming a world-changer starts with something much more powerful than that: a broken heart. Every once in a while you see something and you have to say, "That's enough. Someone needs to take some action here, and they need to do it now." At least that's what happened with Maggie and me. Seeing her was the start of this incredible journey. I didn't know where I was going, but I knew there would be no turning back. I had to do something. I had to help. I was only nine, but so was she. If I waited till I was a grown-up to help, Maggie and millions of other children would be gone.

It was really quiet in our family room when the narrator on the video made his closing comments. It felt really dark when the last images of Africa faded out. Then two last sentences appeared on the screen:

You have one life.

Do something.

My dad turned off the video. But I couldn't turn off what was going on in my heart.

As I slid into my bed that night, safe and warm in a house full of family, tears started streaming down my cheeks. Somewhere, on the other side of the world, maybe Maggie was crying too as she was getting up to face another day.

Take Your Best Shot

Doing something bigger than yourself must begin with the belief that God wants to use you to make a difference. Check out Ephesians 2:10; it says:

> For we are God's masterpiece. He has created us anew in Christ Jesus, so we can do the good things he planned for us long ago.

What do you think about that verse?

Have you had a Maggie Moment yet? When you close your eyes and think of someone in need, whose face do you see?

Do you think God can use you to make a difference in this world and in eternity?

Online: If you want to see *Maggie's Story* for yourself, go to www.youtube.com/hoopsofhope and click on the Videos link. It takes less than four minutes to watch, but be careful—she just might touch your heart and change everything for you too.

chapter 2

Expired Milk

"all that is not eternal is eternally out of date."

{ c. s. lewis, author of
the chronicles of narnia }

I magine eating the best chocolate chip cookie ever. The taste of the warm and chewy dough and melted chocolate chips can only be washed down with one thing—milk. You open the refrigerator door, grab the jug of milk, pour it into a cold glass, and take a drink. As soon as it hits your tongue, you realize you have a mouthful of bitter, sour, and rotten milk.

What comes to mind when you think of expired milk? When I even *think* about expired milk, I immediately get a sour taste in my mouth and a weird shiver that runs up my spine. I almost get a gag reflex. I have to shake it off to try and get it out of my mind. But that's a little bit hard to do, isn't it? It's hard to *not* think about it, especially if you have had the unfortunate experience of accidentally drinking expired milk.

What does expired milk have to do with taking your best shot? Well, the other day I was drinking some chocolate milk, and as I went to put it away, I saw the expiration date. Thankfully, the milk hadn't gone bad yet.

But it made me think about rotten, expired milk. You see, expiration dates are on almost everything, not just milk. Almost everything on this earth will one day be gone. My dog, my house, my computer, my iPod, my basketball, even my cell phone (especially when I forget to take it out of my pocket and it goes through the wash . . . twice). I'm not sure that any of us really believe that someday almost everything on this earth will expire, not just milk. Sure, sometimes we might believe it a little—like the other day when one of my fish died. We had a memorial service in the bathroom just before I flushed the toilet. It was sad. Well, not really. I'm not that attached to my fish, and the memorial service was really an attempt to make my sister laugh. It worked. But the truth is, about thirty seconds after bidding my little fish farewell, I forgot he (or she . . . how do you tell with a fish?) ever existed.

The fact is, most of us are swept away in the flow of life, never really thinking about where we are going or why. We get to thinking that all the stuff around us is really important, when none of it can last anyway. Just like my fish, everything is waiting to get sucked down the toilet in one big swirling swoosh.

Well, *almost* everything.

There is one thing that doesn't. That's us. We're not expired milk. I think that so many times we get caught up in living in the moment that we never really think about two things:

1. We never really think about the fact that someday our bodies will die.
2. We don't realize that the time we have on this earth is really short compared to eternity.

When I think of eternity and how our life on earth measures up to it, I think of the ocean. If you were to throw a rock out into the ocean, you might be able to throw it a few feet. Or maybe you have a better arm than I do, and you can actually throw it pretty far! The distance you are able to throw the rock represents your life in comparison to eternity, which is the huge ocean that goes beyond your throw. When you look at the ocean from the shore, it seems endless. Or think about the sand under your feet as you look out at the sea. Your life could be represented by one little grain of sand. And eternity? It's *all* of the other grains of sand on the beach *and more*.

We have so much more coming up after this. Life doesn't end here. We don't expire, ever. And how we spend our lives can make a difference for eternity. God has a plan for our life here and now. So instead of living like we have an expiration date, don't you think it's time to make an impact and work for things that will last forever?

What's going to last? God and people. That's it. Everything else turns into expired milk.

> **Taking Her Best Shot:**

Ayla

Texas, United States of America

If you passed Ayla in the hall between classes, you'd probably think that she's just an ordinary high school senior. In many ways she is. But in one way, she isn't ordinary at all. Ayla has no idea what the future holds for her on this earth, or even if she *does* have a future on this earth. She explains:

By the grace of God, I am who I am today. I am not the same person I used to be. In 2004 I was diagnosed with a cancer called Hodgkin's Lymphoma. Despite the many chemotherapy treatments I received, the cancer would always return. One day while I was in the hospital, I thought I officially hit rock bottom when my boyfriend of two years broke up with me. But I fell even deeper when a few days later I was informed my cancer returned. The reality of death finally struck me. I was convinced that I was meant to die. Lying in bed, the same questions kept circulating through my mind and through my prayers:

Why am I here?

What is the meaning of life?

Why is this happening to me?

One night God graciously answered those prayers in a life-changing way. It was as if the blinders were removed from my eyes, and suddenly everything made sense. He revealed to me that life is meaningless apart from God. At that moment a joy of joys filled my being, and the burden of sin and my oppression was lifted off me by Christ Jesus. I no longer live for myself as I used to. I was once walking on a path toward destruction, but now I walk on the path of righteousness for the One who mercifully saved me from my sin and hopelessness. In John 6:27 (NIV), Jesus said, "Do not work for food that spoils, but for food that endures to eternal life, which the Son of Man will give you." Being face to face with God and the future eternity is all I look forward to now. To some that may seem foolish, but to the regenerated heart it means everything. Every day *that goes by, I'm reminded that I must live for others and for the eternity that awaits me, because one day I know my time here on earth will be through. Cancer came to me as a curse, but God has made it into a blessing.*

I'm doing all I can to live this life to the fullest. This life isn't about me, it's about Christ, it's about being a "living sacrifice" for Him and for others. Don't waste your life; live it to serve.

Today, Ayla is taking her best shot. She leads a Bible study on her campus and shares her faith with just about anything that breathes. She is passionate about studying the Bible and growing in a deeper relationship with God. She's doing something bigger than herself, and she's doing it today because she knows that she might not have a tomorrow.

Tangled Up in the Temporary

Everything is temporary except God and people. The problem is that there are a lot of people who don't want us to think that way. They want us to focus on things that will expire. Why? Because they make a ton of money off of us, that's why. There are about 33 million of us teenagers in the United States. We spend about $150 billion a year on ourselves, and we influence another $200 billion of the money that our parents spend![2] Each year we are bombarded with millions of advertisements telling us we need the latest and the greatest of whatever it is they are selling. In fact, they intentionally put expiration dates on most of this stuff so that they can sell to us over and over again. They intentionally designed this year's game system to be outdated next year. They make sure the style of clothing they tell us is "in" this fall will be "out" by next fall when it is time to buy your school clothes again. Just pull out some of your parents' old school pictures, and you'll see what I'm talking about. They know that if they can get us to focus our passion on things that will not last, they can keep selling us the same stuff over and over again.

When my dad was my age, someone actually came up with a "toy" called the Pet Rock. Can you believe it? They put a rock in a box and sold it! Guess what? They sold a ton of them. Whenever my dad starts talking about "The Good Ol' Days" and how kids were so much smarter back then, I love to say two simple words to him: Pet Rock!

It's time to quit buying. No, I don't mean we have to

quit buying things, but we need to stop buying into the idea that things that expire are more important than the things that do not expire. Don't let that idea pass by. It's seriously important because, to be honest, the stuff that expires doesn't satisfy anyway. I mean, do *things* ever really make you feel good in the long run? No, they don't. Most of the time they just fuel your hunger for more—a better cell phone, more shoes, the latest gaming system . . . it never ends.

What if we gave to others as much as we give to ourselves? What if we invested as much—or even more—into other people, than we do into ourselves? How would that change your day? Or your life? I wonder what would happen if people put as much effort and money into things that never expire as they did into that Pet Rock?

Pretty simple, isn't it?

Here are a few more things to think about:

» Am I *really* not going to ever expire?
» Is my life on earth *really* that short compared to eternity?
» Does eternity *really* go on forever?
» Is it *really* true that only God and people will exist forever?

» Is everything else *really* going down the toilet?

» Was there *really* such a thing as a Pet Rock?

The answer to these questions, in order, is *really* yes, yes, yes, yes, yes, and, unfortunately, yes.

Now, as long as you're thinking, let me throw one more *really* uncomfortable question your way:

» Am I living for something that will last for eternity?

(The answer to that question may or may not be obvious. Only you know for sure.)

Let me take a shortcut and get right to the point on this. Here's the deal: Everybody lives for something. And everybody is going to die someday. I think it's a tragedy that many people die without ever asking or answering for themselves if what they are living for will last. I can't imagine what it would be like to leave this world and still be wondering: *What was that all about?*

I know it sounds morbid, but seriously, we need to take our best shot at life now because we only get one shot at it. Period. We play the game once, and when the buzzer sounds, we are done on this planet. The only things that matter when we head into the locker room of eternity are the things we invested in that do not expire. God wants us to make a difference in our world—a difference that is going to last. He wants to use us to make a difference to real people who are in real need, right now. That's what drives us on in the journey to do something bigger than ourselves.

And I think that's what moved me to do something about Maggie.

The Phone Call

Maggie's Story kept replaying in my mind. My nine-year-old brain was trying to make sense of what I had seen, but in all honesty, I was having a really tough time processing it all. Weeks and months went by, but I just couldn't shake it. I knew I had to do something, but I didn't know what.

One day my dad took action. He set up a lunch meeting with a guy from World Vision and said, "Hey, we got your video. It rocked my son's world. The rest of us thought it was pretty moving, definitely touching, but it hit Austin pretty hard. In fact, for three months, almost every day he has bugged me to do something about what we watched. Do you guys have any programs for a nine-year-old? Is there anything that children can do? Do you think he could sell Pet Rocks and send the money to Maggie?" (Okay, he didn't say that last part, but it would have been hilarious if he did.)

Long silence.

"How old?"

"Nine," my dad said. "I know you guys have the Thirty-Hour Famine fund-raiser for teenagers. Don't you have like a Two-Hour Famine that you can do with kids?"

Long silence.

"How old?"

"Nine."

"Nothing that I know of, but let me check. I've got a buddy that works up at headquarters. He has a couple of kids, and he's good with them. He'll talk to your son."

When the phone call came in, I was watching the Disney Channel. (I was actually watching *Kim Possible*, but give me a break. I was only nine, okay? Don't tell me you've never watched an episode!) Even before my mom handed me the phone, I knew who it was. I had been waiting and waiting for the call.

"Austin? My name is Dana Buck. . . ."

In all honesty, I don't remember all the details about what he said after that. He did ask me a lot of questions about what was bugging me, about what I was feeling and thinking, and about why I felt like I had to do something.

"Well, Austin, what do you like to do?" he finally asked.

"Ummm, I like sports," I told him. "My favorite sport is basketball."

"Then go out and use basketball to change the world," he said.

I had no clue how a basketball in America could help someone in Africa (neither did anybody else for that matter), but if Mr. Buck said my favorite sport could help the Maggies of the world, that was good enough for me.

This is Dana and I in front of the plaque at the new clinic Hoops of Hope built in Sinazongwe, Zambia.

And then Mr. Buck hung up. (Three years later, as we were standing together on the shores of Lake Kariba in southern Zambia looking for crocodiles, he finally confessed that he never expected to hear from that little nine-year-old kid again.) None of us, not me, not my parents, not Dana . . . no one had a clue what this all meant. How in the world could something that was going to expire (like a sport) be used to make a difference that would last for eternity (like helping AIDS orphans in Africa)? Nobody knew. Nobody except God, that is. God knew that hope could be round and wrapped in leather. He knew that this one phone call was the beginning of Hoops of Hope.

Take Your Best Shot

You are not going to expire. Your life will continue into eternity even though everything else on this earth (except God and other people) is going to get flushed. Thinking about that—I mean *really* thinking about it—can change the course of your life. Consider John 6:27–29:

> "But don't be so concerned about perishable things like food. Spend your energy seeking the eternal life that

the Son of Man can give you. For God the Father has given me the seal of his approval."

They replied, "We want to perform God's works, too. What should we do?"

Jesus told them, "This is the only work God wants from you: Believe in the one he has sent."

Think about that passage and how it relates to "expired milk" and this chapter. What are some things in your life that you're too focused on that will expire?

What are some things you spend time on that will not expire?

Online: Check out the Hoops of Hope blog at www.hoopsofhope.org, and post some comments! You'll also get to read about our most recent adventures in Africa.

Take Action: Do you know someone like Ayla who is struggling with a serious disease? Make them a card or send them an e-mail to let them know you are praying for them. Include verses of encouragement like Psalm 30:2:

O Lord my God, I cried to you for help, and you restored my health.

Chapter 3

Reflections

"everyone thinks of changing the world, but
no one thinks of changing himself."

{ leo tolstoy }

Africa. When I close my eyes, I can remember. I can still see the way the sun rises and sets with the colors of fire on the horizon, and the ripples in the hazy air from the heat. I can still smell the ground beneath my feet and taste the desert dust on my tongue and feel my skin start to moisten with sweat as the new day begins. I can hear the silence of the place, with no electricity humming or cars whooshing past on a highway. I only hear the sounds of God's great creation.

But it's all like a dream now. I have to close my eyes to remember because it's so far away from what I know, so unlike anything else I've ever experienced.

The first time my dad and I went to Africa, we would bounce down these endlessly long dusty roads in trucks. Every time we would stop for water or fuel, tons of kids would gather around to figure out who the strangers were. I wasn't just a stranger—to them, with my super fair skin, red hair, and freckles, I was just plain strange! I was as different to them as Africa was to me. For fun, my dad would take his camera and snap a picture of the kids and then turn the camera around so they could see themselves. Click. Click. Click. These kids loved it. Pretty soon there would be a big line of kids waiting to get their picture taken. What was the big deal about this?! One of the World Vision workers told us that most of the kids had never seen what they look like.

Can you imagine that? Not even knowing what you look like? It seems almost impossible, but it's true. They don't have any mirrors; they don't have pictures; they

My dad was able to show the children their reflection—some for the very first time.

don't have cameras or cell phones to aim at themselves. The best that most of them have is their reflection in water. My dad was able to make a difference in their lives by doing something as simple as showing them their own image. Amazing.

Keep that thought in your mind for just a minute—those kids seeing themselves for the very first time. That's a little funny, isn't it? Because here in America, we have the exact opposite problem. *We are so used to seeing who we are on the* outside *that we never find out who we are on the* inside. But what's on the inside (in our soul and spirit) is what truly matters. You must know what you "look like" on the inside if you are going to take your best shot at something bigger than yourself. One of the mottos at Hoops of Hope and around our house is this:

It's not about what you do.
It's about who you are that matters.

It's Not What You Do

Who are you? Do you really know? If someone asks you that question, you will probably answer with what you *do*:

- » What you *do* have
- » What you *do* look like
- » What you *do*

Let's face it, that's how the whole world looks at you too. Have you ever heard a conversation between two adults meeting each other? You can almost guarantee that this will be one of their first questions: "So, what do you do for a living?" (Someday, if I get asked that question, I'm going to say I raise Pet Rocks.) If you do the right things, have the right stuff, and wear the right look—then you're popular. But if you don't do the right things, and you don't have the right stuff, you will quickly find yourself on the outside of the "in" crowd. (Unless you have the right looks, of course. For whatever reason, if you've got the right looks, you can get away with almost anything.)

That stinks. Because it's what you have on the inside that matters. It truly is. If you're going to do something bigger than yourself, you'll need to start thinking differently than the world thinks, and you'll need to start thinking that way now.

A group of students was once asked to pick the

current Seven Wonders of the World. Each student got to answer once, and then they tallied all their answers to come up with a combined list of great human accomplishments—the Great Pyramids, the Panama Canal, the Empire State Building, St. Peter's Basilica, the Taj Mahal, the Grand Canyon, and the Great Wall of China. (If you ask me, the invention of the Extra-Long Chili Cheese Coney Dog should have made the list, but nobody was asking me.)

One quiet girl sitting in the back didn't respond. The teacher asked her if she were having trouble. "There are just too many. I can't decide," she said. "Well, tell us what you have, and maybe we can help you choose," the teacher said. The little girl hesitated and then read, "I think the present seven wonders of the world are:

- » to see,
- » to hear,
- » to touch,
- » to taste,
- » to run,
- » to laugh, and . . .
- » to love."[3]

Wow, that's a really different kind of list, isn't it? While everyone in the class focused on what human beings *do*, this wise little girl was blown away by who human beings *are*. And she was right. You see, it's what's on the inside that really matters. The little girl focused on who she was as God created her to be and what she had to offer because . . .

It's not about what you do.
It's about who you are that matters.

It's all a matter of focus. If we focus on what we do, it all becomes about *us*. If we focus on who we are, then suddenly it all becomes about *God*.

Who You Are

So, how do we focus on who we are? Remember my dad taking pictures of little kids in Africa? His camera showed the kids what they look like on the outside. The Bible works that way for us too, except that it shows us what we're like on the inside—all the good and all the bad. It's like God takes a little camera deep inside of us and goes "Click. Click. Click." Then he turns the camera around and shows us what's going on inside of our soul and inside of our spirit. Like those little kids in Africa, there's a good chance we have never seen this stuff before. Just like my dad was able to make a difference in their lives doing something as simple as showing them their own image, God can transform our lives when he shows us what is true about us on the inside. That is our real reflection, not the face in the mirror.

If you were to take a picture of yourself, on the inside, what would you see? Hurt, fear, selfishness, pride, lone-liness? Would you see someone who doesn't have any self-esteem? Would you see someone who doesn't have anyone to say they love you, to tell you they're proud of you? Now take a look at three other pictures.

Picture #1: Forgiven

> If we confess our sins to him, he is faithful and just to forgive us our sins and to cleanse us from all wickedness. —1 John 1:9

This one is huge. Society judges you by what you do. And when you blow it? You're pretty much done. You get "punished" in a lot of different ways—including being rejected and made fun of. Most people have a hard time getting past their mistakes. They either hold on to them or other people hold on to them. God is different. No matter what you do or don't do, when you ask for forgiveness, you *are* forgiven by him. That's what the cross is about. Jesus took the punishment for everything you have done wrong—the little things and the huge things— so that you can have a close personal friendship with God. "So now there is no condemnation for those who belong to Christ Jesus" (Romans 8:1). Oh, and when Jesus forgives you . . . he really forgives you. In fact, the Bible says that he separates our sins from us as far as the east is from the west (Psalm 103:12), that he remembers them no more. Is that a great picture or what?!

Picture #2: Adopted

> So you have not received a spirit that makes you fearful slaves. Instead, you received God's Spirit when he adopted you as his own children. Now we call him, "Abba, Father." For his Spirit joins with our spirit to affirm that we are God's children.
> —Romans 8:15–16

Not only does God forgive you, he totally accepts you. He opens up his arms and gives you this huge hug, and he looks in your eyes with a gaze of perfect love and says, "You are totally mine now. I'm your dad, and you are my kid. Nothing you do, nothing that you don't do will ever, ever change that. You *are* mine."

Picture #3: Transformed

> I stopped trying to meet all [the law's] requirements. . . . My old self has been crucified with Christ. It is no longer I who live, but Christ lives in me. —Galatians 2:19-20

This is where the picture of what's going on inside you gets interesting. The Bible says that you are fearfully and wonderfully made. You are made in the image of God himself. He has put his fingerprint on you, and with that fingerprint you can do incredible things. Why? Because the Spirit of God and Jesus actually live in you. You've been transformed by God. When God is in your life, he is really *in* your life.

Do you believe that? You'll probably have to think about this for as long as you live. I sure do. Yet I can't tell you how important it is to believe this and to act on it if you really want to take your best shot and really do something bigger than yourself. *Because doing something bigger than yourself truly requires having Someone bigger than yourself inside you!* Do you get that?

It's not what you do; it's who you are—on the *inside*.

Imagine those little kids in Africa seeing themselves for the first time. You think they believed it? Do you think they truly believed that was who they were? They had to look at the screen several times. At first we might not believe what the Bible says is true about us either. But this is who we truly are. We are forgiven, adopted, and transformed by the Spirit of God in us.

If you don't like the picture you see of yourself, if you don't feel like you have worth or value, all of that can change. Or maybe you do realize your worth, but you feel like maybe there's more to life than what you've got. The good news is that all you have to do is ask, and Christ will come into your life. He can transform your life and equip you with everything you need to live a fulfilled life now and for eternity! Here's what Jesus tells us:

"Look! I stand at the door and knock. If you hear my voice and open the door, I will come in, and we will share a meal together as friends." —Revelation 3:20

Take Your Best Shot

Here are some questions to think about:

Forgiven:
Are you forgiven? You can be. Just tell God you know you've messed up, and you're sorry. Then thank him for forgiving you for all the wrong things in your life.

Adopted:
Do you believe you've been adopted? If you have asked Christ to come into your life, to forgive you, and to help you with the things you still struggle with, you've become one of his kids. He's a great Father—one who'll never leave you. Thank him for accepting you just the way you are.

Transformed:
Have you let him transform you? Tell Christ you want him to

come into your life on every level, that you want his Spirit living in you. Thank him for doing that and for never leaving you or turning his back on you. Now you can make a difference— *because he is in you!*

> This means that anyone who belongs to Christ has become a new person. The old life is gone; a new life has begun! And all of this is a gift from God, who brought us back to himself through Christ.
> —2 Corinthians 5:17–18

Write your own personal prayer to God.

Online: Do you have pictures that show who you *are*? And how you're working to make a difference in the world? Sign on to Facebook and post them on the Hoops of Hope group page! You can also check out photos from our trips to Africa at www.hoopsofhope.org. Click the Follow tab and then the Flickr link.

Chapter 4

Just Another Kid

"we're too young to realize that certain things are impossible! so we will do them anyway!"

{ young william pitt to william wilberforce in the movie *amazing grace* }

Do you know what the big difference is between an adult and a kid? Their age. Yep, that's it. Brilliant, huh?

I'm serious about it, though. The biggest difference between us and them is that they have existed longer than we have. If you put adults into a new situation, something they've never experienced, they'd respond pretty much like we would.

I learned this our first night in Africa. We were spending the night in one of the World Vision offices. (This was our normal mode of operation. We called it "office camping.") We had climbed onto our floor mattresses and were getting ready to call it a night when we saw this monster spider on the ceiling. No joke, it was at least four inches across. Huge, hairy, and ugly—kind of like a Chihuahua, except with more hair. Every man in the room let out a yell—it sounded like a bunch of screaming Girl Scouts. (Okay, so I yelled too, but that's not the point here.) So the yelling spooked the spider, and it fell onto this dude's pillow with a thud. I mean, it was so big, you could hear it land. While everybody tried to find a sledgehammer or steamroller or some-thing to squish it with, the spider looked around like he was wondering, *Wow, what's with all the new guys in town?* And then it cruised down the hall and took a left out the door, like it knew exactly where it was going. I'm telling you, every man in that room was freaking out because we figured the Chihuahua spider had friends. It was probably inviting them to come back over for a midnight snack. My point? Whether you're fourteen or thirty-nine, new experiences often affect us in the same way. And enormous spiders make every-one scream.

The same is true for taking your best shot. Any time someone does something the first couple of times, it's going to be awkward and scary . . . no matter how old you are. But after you've done it a couple of times? It will seem like old hat, and you'll be ready to take on a new challenge. Later in the trip, we were setting up camp in a small lodge when one of the guys noticed three spiders on the ceiling. (Three spiders at four inches per spider equals one foot, by the way . . . and you thought math was worthless.) But by that point in the trip, we'd seen so many that nobody really thought about it. It was more like, "As long as that thing doesn't try to kick me off my cot and steal my backpack or something, no big deal."

If you think making a difference is going to be any easier when you're an adult, you're mistaken. Doing something new that's bigger than yourself doesn't depend on how *old* you are. It depends on how *available* you are. If you choose to be available, God will work through you even if you are young, and even if you are just a "regular" person. I think kids have an advantage over adults, actually. Adults have had a lot longer to get discouraged and distracted, and many of them have learned to doubt whether or not they can make the world a better place. Kids? We don't know any better.

Believe me, I'm not downplaying the fact that taking your best shot is scary. What I am saying is that it makes no difference that you are young or that you are not a superstar. (It doesn't matter if you are old and "regular" either!) The fact is that God wants to use you. But sometimes that means you might have to stare a giant in the eye.

David, Just Another Kid

There are certain stories that stir up something inside of you. Stories that get you pumped up and make you want to take your best shot. The story of David does that for me. Here's the deal:

In 1 Samuel chapter 17 the Israelite army (good guys) is having a stare-down with the Philistine army (bad guys). The Philistines have a monster All-Star on their side: Goliath, who measures in at over nine feet tall. (He was big *and* bad—and probably hairy.) The Israelites, understandably, are freaked out about this (wimpy good guys, go figure). Goliath keeps challenging them, telling them that he will fight anybody one-on-one, winner take all. (The losing army would become the slaves of the winners.) For some reason, nobody on the Israelite side feels like having their arms ripped off and getting killed by Goliath. So every day Goliath comes out and insults God and taunts the Israelites. David, who's just a shepherd boy at the time (most Bible scholars say he was between twelve and fourteen years old), wanders into the camp one day and sees all this going on.

But he sees things differently. He doesn't see this as one man fighting another; he sees that this is a God thing—it's Goliath against *God* . . . and David knows who's bigger. He believes that God wants to use him to make a difference in this situation. But the Israelites don't take David seriously at all. After all, he's just another kid, right? And who can blame them? They were looking at what David could do (a scrawny kid facing a freak of nature). But David knew who he was, and he knew who God was, and he had had enough of the Philistines talking down about his God.

The Israelites don't have the guts to face Goliath themselves, and they are pretty sure David is going to get squished. So they try to dress him up in a bunch of heavy armor and arm him with the weapons they use. (Just like a lot of well-meaning adults might tell you how and when you should do things when you're trying to help others. They might try to get you to do it their way, or pressure you to wait until after you graduate, or go to college, or get married, and so on.) Turns out, David can hardly move in the heavy armor or even lift the weapons. He drops their plan and goes into battle just as he is.

David squares off with Goliath. Goliath looks at this little shepherd, and they start talking trash. Goliath says, "Come over here, and I'll give your flesh to the birds and wild animals!" (1 Samuel 17:44). (Most guys would have headed back to the locker room to change their underwear, but not David. He's got God on his side, and he knows it.) David shouts back, "You come to me with sword, spear, and javelin, but I come to you in the name of the LORD . . . This is the LORD's battle, and he will give you to us!" (1 Samuel 17:45-47). Goliath moves closer to attack. David sprints toward him carrying the only "weapon" that he knows how to use—a slingshot and five small stones.

And when David slings the stone, God drops the giant with a mighty thud.

Carpe Diem (Seize the Day)

After I took the call from Dana at World Vision, I felt immediately energized, like David must have felt while staring down Goliath. The problem of AIDS orphans stood like a foul-mouthed giant, a hairy Chihuahua spider, taunting me to do something about it. But the problem seemed too big. *What could anyone do about millions of kids without parents, struggling for life? What could I do?* The answer, realistically, was nothing. I was just a kid after all. I was going to use a basketball to fight AIDS? Yeah, right. That's totally insane when you think about it. I was confused. But I knew God was speaking to me, and I knew my love for basketball had something to do with what he was saying. One of the reasons I was confused was because even though I love basketball, I stink at it. There are people who are worse than I am, for sure, but to be honest, the only reason I made the basketball team when I was younger was because my dad was the coach. One year I gave my all for the whole season . . . and I made *one* point—a free throw in the last game. I've never been as good at basketball as other people, and I'm still not.

But it doesn't matter.

You don't have to be extraordinary; you just have to be willing. You don't have to wait to be an adult to make a difference and, if you are an adult, it's never too late to begin to think like a kid. But be warned, it's sometimes really hard for adults to think like that. My dad was out of town on business when Dana and I talked on the phone. When he got home, I told him everything I could remember from the call. I told him that I was going to go out and play basketball for these kids. He smiled politely and patted me on the head. "Oh. Okay. That sounds great, buddy." That's what everyone said. That's probably what they told David too, "Great, buddy. We will scrape up what's left of you when the giant has had his way . . ."

But you know what? I didn't even care that no one else was into it. I guess I just wasn't old enough to know how weird it was. I just knew I had to do something, and for some reason I believed that God could use me to do whatever that "something" was. My God is David's God. If David used a slingshot, couldn't I use a basketball?

> **Taking Their Best Shot:**

Lifetime Caring Orphanage Home

Nigeria, Africa

The leaders of the Lifetime Caring Orphanage Home in Nigeria have a powerful goal. They're trying to build: *A*

world in which every woman, girl, man and boy can ex-
ercise their right to a life of dignity. The kids there are
taking their best shot to achieve it. As Rev. Lucky Suanu
Abaadan, who heads the orphanage, put it, "We have
been mandated by the almighty God to help with compassion, those who have been forgotten by the society,
the less privileged, orphans, widows, youth, prisoners,
and sick people."

What is one thing they decided to do to fulfill that
vision? They decided to shoot hoops! They sponsored a
Hoops of Hope event for another orphanage that was
caring for motherless babies and young children.

Can you imagine? Orphans caring for other orphans?
The kids at this orphanage prove that you don't have to
have a lot in order to give big. You just need a big heart
and the willingness to go out and make a difference.

Back in Zambia

The day after our encounter with the monster spider,
we drove four hours into a little village that seemed to
be in the middle of nowhere. Sitting in another relief

agency office, we were hearing of things that were far more scary than our hairy eight-legged friend from the night before. A World Vision worker named Clement Chipollilo and three other aid workers told us about what was happening in the region. There are no factories and no businesses. When we asked how many people had jobs, he just kind of laughed. There are no jobs. Everyone tries to live off the land. They plant crops and then they hope that they will grow, but they are in the middle of a fifteen-year drought that has basically destroyed anything that grows in the land. Pneumonia has killed almost all of the cattle. But that's not the worst of it.

The worst part is the children who are being left behind by AIDS. When a child's parents die, the nearest relatives try to take the child if they can afford it. If they can't afford it or when those relatives die, the children are left at the mercy of others in the village. The five men who were working out of that office, Clement included, were raising thirty-five children besides their own. That's the reality in the villages. But that's still not the worst of it. "In the city," they told us, "children must raise themselves. You will see them along the streets. Kids raising kids as best they

All of these children lived with their grandmother in a small house.

can. The oldest becomes the head of the household. Because they have no one and nothing. They are just kids."

It's too horrible to even imagine. I tried to grasp what he was telling us, but it was just too much to absorb. Someone asked Clement the age of the youngest head of a household that he knew of.

"She is seven years old," he said. "She tries to take care of her brothers and sisters as best she can. What else can she do?"

Seven years old. Seven years old. Just a kid.

55

Don't let anyone tell you that kids can't make a difference. Can you make a difference even if you are "just a kid"? Absolutely. No matter where you are, no matter what your skills are, no matter what your age is, you can make a difference. With God, *all* things are possible.

That little girl in Zambia is making a difference because she *has* to. We can make a difference because we *choose* to.

Take Your Best Shot

Spend some time with God talking about these two passages in the Bible:

I know how to live on almost nothing or with everything. I have learned the secret of living in every situation, whether it is with a full stomach or empty, with plenty or little. For I can do everything through Christ, who gives me strength. —Philippians 4:12–13

This is why we work hard and continue to struggle, for our hope is in the living God, who is the Savior of all people and particularly of all believers.

Teach these things and insist that everyone learn them. Don't let anyone think less of you because you are young.

Be an example to all believers in what you say, in the way you live, in your love, your faith, and your purity. —1 Timothy 4:10–12.

Some people believe that you have to be an adult to make a difference. Do you think that's true?

Have you ever felt that some people look at you as if you are "just a kid"? When?

If you could do anything in the world to help people, what would it be?

Take Action: A lot of children in Africa are taking care of their siblings because they have to—they are their only providers. Help your parents out today by taking care of younger siblings. Play a game, watch a movie, or spend some time together outside.

Chapter 5

First Things First

"do not have your concert first, and then tune
your instrument afterwards. begin the day
with the Word of God and prayer, and get first
of all into harmony with him."

{ hudson taylor, missionary to china }

The pavement always ends just beyond the city limits. From there on out, it's nothing but dirt and wind and sun. Forget about rest areas or truck stops or taking the exit ramp to the nearest fast-food joint. You'll find none of that in Zambia. Once the city is in your rearview mirror, it's like you're driving into nowhere—and the next somewhere can be a long, long way away.

If you get lost out there, you're history. No one

We stopped for a rest on the side of a dusty African road.

would have a clue about where to start looking. And who would look for you anyway? There's no highway patrol or sheriff; no one who would even know you were missing. Most roads are not much more than trails that snake across the plains in a random maze that connects one village to the next. It's a vast and dangerous land, and I have to be honest—I love it.

Once, we stopped out in the middle of nowhere to take a break. We just pulled over to the side of the road. I heard a few young voices and laughter in the bushes and went over to find three girls giggling and spying on us. I coaxed them out with a few pieces of candy, and we communicated through our smiles and gestures as best we could. Shyly, they showed me the "toy" they had been playing with. It was a simple block of wood. In a few moments, we were back on the road kicking up more dust into the African sky. I kept wondering, *Who were those girls? What was their story? What were they doing out in the middle of nowhere?* I'll never know, but I'll also never forget them.

You never know what kind of adventure awaits you on the roads of Zambia. But there is one thing I know for sure: if you don't keep first things first, you'll never complete the journey. Here in America, you can take

These are the little girls we found, literally, in the middle of nowhere.

off driving and plan later. Not so over there. If you don't prepare properly, you are going to end up as buzzard food. The most important commandment for anyone who travels in remote Africa is *you must have a continual supply of gasoline, and you must have water.* Those two things are in very short supply outside of the cities, and if you run out, it's all over. Most vehicles that travel through the wild always start with a full tank of gas and plenty of extra jugs of water. Those who are wise also carry extra gas in spare tanks strapped on the back. They know that nothing is more important for physical survival.

The Greatest Command

As followers of God who want to take our best shot and do something bigger than ourselves, we have a similar commandment. Nothing is more important to our survival. It sounds so simple, but it's absolutely essential to making a difference. Jesus said:

> "You must love the LORD your God with all your heart, all your soul, and all your mind." This is the first and greatest commandment. —Matthew 22:37–38

Well-known passages like this one are kind of like car alarms. I remember when I was a little kid, and I heard a car alarm for the first time. When I heard that loud, honking, screeching siren, I was convinced my neighbor's car was getting broken into. As it turned out, they had just accidentally hit the "panic" button on the key remote. Of course some car alarms *are* set off by burglars, but most are set off by accident. Here's my point: we hear car alarms all the time, so much in fact that they've sort of lost their impact. If you're like me, when you hear a car alarm you don't even look to see if anything is wrong anymore. (Usually it's just my dad hitting the button on purpose so he can find his car in the parking lot!) We have become numb to something that used to be really important. All because we've heard it so many times!

Sometimes we do the same with this command to love God. But if we ignore this command, we miss the entire adventure of life! This is the *key* to life—and you don't use it just once; you use this key all the time. Loving God constantly opens up the door to life as God created it to be lived. The most important thing, the first thing above all else, is a loving friendship and a close relationship between you and God. We are called to love God with everything we have. This is the fuel for the fire, the oxygen in the lungs, the blood that beats in the heart. For anyone who wants to take their best shot and do something bigger than themselves, *loving God is the gas in the tank and the water in the jug*. It's that important; it's *the* most important command. Everything else comes in second place.

At Hoops of Hope, we try to remind ourselves of that

all the time. For some reason, God is choosing to use basketballs right now to help kids on the other side of the globe. I don't know why, but I do know that it's not going to last forever. Someday this part of the movement is going to change, one way or the other, but our love for God? I pray that it just keeps on growing because that's the greatest commandment of all.

But there is another commandment too. Jesus said:

> A second is equally important: "Love your neighbor as yourself." —Matthew 22:39

Love Yourself

Love yourself? Is that a mistake? Wasn't I supposed to just write, "Love your neighbor"? All we are supposed to do is to love God and love our neighbors, right? No. Let's look a little more carefully at the rest of the second part of that verse: ". . . love your neighbor *as* yourself." Maybe you've heard that verse a million times, but have you ever really thought about the end of that verse? We all know about the first part. We're supposed to love others. What this verse is saying is that we are supposed to love them on the same level that we love ourselves. So that would require us to first love ourselves so we can love others. In fact, it would appear that the more we love ourselves, the more we will love others.

For many of us, loving ourselves doesn't come very easily. My guess is that a lot of that has to do with the fact that we measure ourselves by the wrong standards. We measure ourselves by what the world says makes somebody "loveable." And when we look in the mirror and see pimples and bad hair; when we see a body that's too tall or too short, or too thick or too thin; when we see a reflection of somebody who isn't as popular or as smart or as athletic or as artistic as we think we should be, we find it tough to love ourselves.

Then, as if that weren't enough, pile on all the dumb stuff we do, and loving ourselves gets even tougher. Believe me, there are a lot of days I wish I were taller or had six-pack abs. But what if I were taller, more buff, and more athletic? What if I never made any stupid mistakes? What if you or I had all the qualities we think we should have? It wouldn't matter. Because that's not what it's about. Trust me. The most beautiful girl and the best-looking guy you know have things about themselves that they don't like.

Here's the deal: God doesn't look at us the way we do. We aren't talking about what we look like on the outside or what we do, we're talking about who we are. When we can begin to see ourselves the way God sees us, we may find it easier to love ourselves. And in order to take your best shot, you need to love who God created you to be. God loves you so much that he was willing to come to earth as a man and die on the cross for you. He totally accepts you just as you are, and he thinks you're great! If God loves you like this, what's stopping you from loving yourself? *Do you think you have higher standards than he does?!* The fact is that God is crazy about you. And he needs you to love yourself so you can go out and show his love to others.

You might not feel great about yourself, but there comes a time when you have to *accept* what God says is true, and then *act* on that even if you don't feel like it.

» You might feel like you are rejected and unacceptable. But God totally accepts you and thinks you're completely worthy of his love:

Therefore, accept each other just as Christ has accepted you so that God will be given glory.
—Romans 15:7

» You might feel like you are alone. But God is always with you and in you:

And I am convinced that nothing can ever separate us from God's love. Neither death nor life, neither angels nor demons, neither our fears for today nor our worries about tomorrow—not even the powers of hell can separate us from God's love. No power in the sky above or in the earth below—indeed, nothing in all creation will ever be able to separate us from the love of God that is revealed in Christ Jesus our Lord. —Romans 8:38-39

» You might feel like a loser who can't do anything right. Let's be honest; we all have those days. But you can do *anything* because of who God has made you to be:

For I can do everything through Christ, who gives me strength. —Philippians 4:13

» You might feel like you can't reach God. But you have direct access to him all the time:

So let us come boldly to the throne of our
gracious God. There we will receive his mercy,
and we will find grace to help us when we
need it most. —Hebrews 4:16

» You might feel like you are weak and have no
strength. But you have the power of God's
Spirit in you:

But you will receive power when the Holy
Spirit comes upon you. And you will be my
witnesses, telling people about me
everywhere—in Jerusalem, throughout Judea,
in Samaria, and to the ends of the earth.
—Acts 1:8

The list goes on and on. The whole Bible is filled
with truths that tell you how lovable and how awesome
you truly are because of what God has done inside you.
That's why "love God" always comes first and "love
yourself" comes second, because when you focus on a
loving relationship with God by spending time listening to his Holy Spirit and his Word, his love begins to
fill you up. Then you're ready to go out and love your

neighbor. You're like a Land Rover with extra gas in the tank and spare water up on top. You're ready for the journey, and you are ready to give. Here are three things that help me love God, love myself, and love my neighbor:

1. Focus Time

God provides special places and times when we can focus just on him. "Focus Time" takes place at church, at youth group, maybe at a Christian concert or at a big conference. And it's great. We learn about him; we worship him. We might even be a part of a massive project working with other people. Most people are pretty good at getting Focus Time with their friends or their family, but it's easy to forget that God deserves Focus Time too.

2. Quiet Time

Our lives are bombarded with noise—TV, teachers, text messages, parents, Facebook, cell phones, blogs, friends, even church stuff. Our brains are constantly attacked with noise from the outside. I think one of the biggest challenges in loving God and loving yourself is overcoming all the noise so we can hear what is going on inside. One of the most important things you can do to keep *first things first* is to take advantage of time alone with God. Just you, God, and a Bible. It's kind of like a date—a date with God (but without the awkward hug good night)—and you can have them as often as you want. "Quiet Time" is when the two of you talk, listen, think, and read the Bible together. If you're going to take your best shot, having Quiet Time with God on a regular basis is one of the most important priorities you can make.

3. All the Time

Now, get this: one of the incredible things about being changed by God and having his Spirit within you is that *anytime is time with him*. You are with God *all the time*. Think about that, because sometimes people think you have to have Focus Time (at church or a camp) or Quiet Time (locked away in a room someplace) in order to "get closer to God." What's amazing is that you really can't get any "closer" to God than you already are! He's right there inside of you all the time. All you have to do is be aware of that and take advantage of it. It's like walking with a best friend, *All the Time*. You can talk to him, share things with him, laugh with him, cry with him *All the Time*. It just doesn't get any better than that.

Use those three kinds of time, and you'll find your love for God growing. As his love overflows into your life, you'll find yourself being able to love yourself like never before. And then, something really crazy starts to happen.

You start to do things that are bigger than yourself.

Love Others

If you keep first things first, loving your neighbor will come naturally. You don't have to force it or make it up. Just know that if you keep first things first, everything else will take care of itself, moment by moment. It goes something like this:

» You might be having some *Focus Time* with God at a camp, and something the speaker says from the Bible really hits home. You feel like God is telling you he wants you to go on an overseas mission trip.

» Or you might be having some *Quiet Time* with God when he reminds you about the verses on purity that your youth pastor talked about this week. You think about how your boyfriend has really been trying to push the limit on your physical boundaries, and you realize that he's not the kind of guy God wants for you.

» You might be having some *All the Time* with God as you walk from class to class. Suddenly you see a teacher who looks like she's having a really rough day. You can feel God's nudge, so you stop to say hello and pay her a compliment. During the conversation, you realize God put you in the right place at the right time to really turn someone's day around.

2,057

Okay, back to Hoops of Hope. It seemed like God had given us the green light to somehow use basketball to help AIDS orphans. But how?

During some Quiet Time with God, I read in James 1:27 where it says, "Pure and genuine religion in the sight of God the Father means caring for orphans and widows in their distress and refusing to let the world corrupt you." It's like God was planting this desire in my heart. I couldn't stop thinking about those kids in Africa. So we kept thinking and praying about ways to help, and God started to make things happen. We were prepared for the journey, and God directed us as we headed down the road. The details just kind of "showed up."

World Vision had a program where people could sign up to run a marathon and get sponsors to help them raise money to sponsor kids like Ignatius and Maggie. I looked at that Web site with my parents, and we thought, *Eww, running? Who wants to do that? Who wants to put their body through that kind of torture?!*

That's the moment it hit me. *What if people sponsored me for shooting basketballs?*

It was so simple, but so perfect. My mom and dad said, "Okay, we will help you set up a Web page. We are totally behind you. Shoot a basket for a buck or something." Yep, my parents were "totally behind me" on this. Later, my dad admitted that he thought the idea was sort of crazy, but he just wanted to encourage me. He thought I'd shoot a few hoops and raise a few bucks for Africa and be done with it. (Note to self: God works in crazy, unusual ways.)

So then I started messing around with a goal.

During *Maggie's Story*, I heard the statistic that six thousand children are orphaned by AIDS every day in Africa. It got me thinking again. *Hmmm. What if I shot one free throw for every one of those kids?* My dad did some quick math in his head and politely told me that was insane. (Six thousand shots divided by eight hours, divided by sixty minutes, equals more than twelve shots per minute or about one shot every five seconds for eight hours straight. Yeah, right. Not possible.) He told me to figure out how many were orphaned in a school day.

I did the math and thought it through. It was like God was saying, "Hey, Austin. Give it your best shot. If it works, we will be able to sponsor eight orphans for a year." That settled it. On December 1, World AIDS Awareness Day, God and I were going to shoot 2,057 free throws. (And I thought *runners* were crazy.)

You know, taking your best shot and doing something bigger than yourself really is a lot like driving through the African plains. It's an adventure all the way, and you never know for sure what's going to happen. There might be detours and ditches and an awful lot of dust along the way, but if you prepare properly, and keep your tank filled by loving God with all your heart, soul, strength, and mind, the details of the journey just seem to take care of themselves.

Take Your Best Shot

Carve out a little bit of Quiet Time when you can be alone with God. Get away from all the noise that usually distracts you, so you can just enjoy your friendship with him. Reread Matthew 22:35–40:

> One of them, an expert in religious law, tried to trap him [Jesus] with this question: "Teacher, which is the most important commandment in the law of Moses?"
>
> Jesus replied, "'You must love the LORD your God with all your heart, all your soul, and all your mind.' This is the first and greatest commandment. A second is equally important: 'Love your neighbor as yourself.' The entire law and all the demands of the prophets are based on these two commandments."

Take Your Best Shot

Really talk to God about this passage. What is he telling you about keeping first things first?

What do you think about this whole idea of loving God, loving yourself, and loving others? What do you think it would be like if you walked with God like this *All the Time*?

Chapter 6

Boomerangs

"the more he cast away, the more he had."

{ british author john bunyan (1628–1688)
in *the pilgrim's progress* }

I'm not even sure why I did it. It just sort of happened. And it sure didn't make sense at the time. We were on the road again in a Land Rover packed full of men with no air-conditioning and the windows down. The only thing worse than the dust was the heat—the kind of heat that makes a bunch of old guys in a Land Rover smell terrible. It was like we were riding in our own personal furnace.

We stopped at a village to get something cold to drink at a local "convenience store." It wasn't much more than a shack, actually, but unlike so many buildings in that part of the country, it did have electricity, which meant that it had a refrigerator! The shopkeeper pulled out bottles of Coke from the rusty, tilting icebox. Sweet, thick, cold—the kind of cold that makes the bottles drip with condensation on the outside.

Outside the store, I was trying to talk with a boy who was about my age. He only spoke Tongan. A translator was helping a little bit, but I really wished I could get into his world and find out more about him. He was barefoot like all the kids, with a dirty shirt and a big bag over his shoulder filled with bottles and cans. Was he trying to recycle them for a little bit of money? Was he going to use them to make toys? I didn't have time to hear his story, but just before we got back in the truck, I felt "the nudge"—a little tug on my heart that seemed to come out of nowhere and certainly made no sense. *Do it, Austin. Trust me. I dare you.* So I did. I gave the boy my Coke and walked back toward the truck empty-handed. Like I said, I'm not even sure why I did it. When I got back into the truck, and we started to roll down the dusty road again, I got this quiet feeling deep down inside—deeper than my dry lips, deeper than my

This is the boy I met in the African village where we stopped for cokes.

stomach, which would have loved the cool blast of sugar. It was the weirdest thing. Something had just happened. Something important . . .

Blessings

Have you ever gotten the feeling that we have it all backward? I mean, we seem to be so sure that things work a certain way, but do they really? What if the way that seems right is really wrong, and what if what seems wrong really is the right way? Take a look at this Bible verse for example:

> And I have been a constant example of how you can help those in need by working hard. You should remember the words of the Lord Jesus: "It is more blessed to give than to receive." —Acts 20:35

More blessed to give than to receive. What? Sorry, but if on Christmas morning, I didn't get anything and my sister loaded up, I'd probably be a bit disappointed. Sure, I'd act happy for her, but deep down inside I'd be bummed. Like that special Christmas morning when my parents decided I would receive clothes instead of toys; I can't say that I was thrilled. I didn't even get a Pet Rock. I mean, we're all human, and we all like to get stuff, which is why phrases like this don't make sense to us. Did Jesus have it backward, or did he know something we don't? What was he trying to teach us? I believe he said what he meant. We are blessed when we give, but not in the way that we would expect.

I think blessings are like boomerangs. You know, that L-shaped, wooden, Frisbee thing? When you throw one of those things, they make this long sweeping arc before they start to turn and come back in your direction. It's so cool to watch. You throw it away from yourself, and then it just seems to come back on its own. At least that's how it works in theory, or if you know what you're doing. For most people, those things hardly ever work. They either come back way too fast and make you duck for cover, or they "come back" to a location about two miles away from where you first tossed it. Sometimes they don't come back at all, and you have to go out and find them.

But giving *always* comes back. It just comes back in a different way. And you know what else? It doesn't just come back different; it comes back *better*. It comes back as a *blessing*. A blessing that is real, deep, and more powerful and profound than anything we could ever get. How does it do that?

Well, for one thing, when you help change someone's life, it changes yours. When Hoops of Hope was getting started, I always thought that I was helping the lives of kids in Africa. *Get a ball, shoot some hoops, and help AIDS orphans in Africa.* It was a pretty simple plan. We were just throwing that boomerang, and I had no idea that it would come back to bless me. But it has. It's a blessing that is bigger than all the cool things I've gotten to do (going to Africa anyone?!), and I think it's all about perspective.

It feels like being two things at once. You feel so small and insignificant when you see how many people need help, and you know that you're only one person in one generation in the whole of eternity (like that grain of sand on the beach). But at the same time, you feel larger than life. God is on our side, binding us all together into one huge web. I know that I'm just one teeny tiny part of that whole, but knowing that I'm part of it has changed me forever. I pray that it has changed all of those who help out with Hoops of Hope.

And another thing: When you listen to God, and give as he leads you, you get this great feeling inside. If you have felt this, you know what I mean. If you haven't, there's really no way to describe it. You have this awesome sense of satisfaction that God used you to help someone. I think that's what was going on in the Land Rover after I gave that kid my drink. Something inside me said, *Yeah, buddy. This is what it's all about. This fits with who you are. This is just right. Thanks for trusting me on this.*

My Best Shot

My life was pretty much consumed with that feeling after I made the decision to shoot the 2,057 free throws. It was just exciting. I felt like I was waiting for my birthday or Christmas all the time. The next step was to try to get the word out and see if I could find enough sponsors to earn one dollar per shot. My parents encouraged me to give it my best, but inside they were skeptical. I sent out a bunch of e-mails asking people to sponsor me on the Web site, and then I started hitting up my relatives. I just kept thinking about those kids in Africa and feeling really, really excited that I had a chance to do something about it. Grandpa and Grandma kicked in, of course. (Grandparents are such easy targets!) And they talked to a lot of their friends too. It was just kind of a chain reaction. The money was coming in. Next up, I had to actually shoot that many free throws. It never crossed my mind that this might be physically impossible. It never crossed my mind that this was the beginning of something bigger. I was just in the moment, doing what I felt I needed to do in a way that I loved. Finally, December 1, World AIDS Awareness Day arrived. I was ready to give it my best shot to make a difference for eight kids for one year.

I don't think the janitor appreciated having to be at the gym early that morning to let us in. (But I think he actually felt blessed later in the day when he realized what he had been a part of!) Some of our close family friends came down to watch me get started. They pulled out an autographed Steve Nash jersey—one of my favorite players in the NBA! I couldn't believe it! I just thought, *There's no way!* If I had been lacking any enthusiasm before, it was totally overflowing after I saw that jersey.

My mom knew I had a long day ahead of me. She did something that has become a tradition at all Hoops of Hope events—she hung a banner behind the basket that said, "Hope for children orphaned by AIDS." I walked up to the free-throw line, bounced the ball once or twice, and let it fly. It was a beautiful sight. I've always loved the way that a free throw arcs through the air on its way to the net. There's just something about that sound as the ball swishes through the net and then drops to the floor. But . . . I didn't get to hear that. I gave it my best shot, and the ball bounced off the rim. My mom went chasing after it. It was the beginning of a long and wonderful day.

Test It

There's no doubt about it in my mind: we are more blessed when we give than when we receive. How does it work? I really don't know, but it does, unless our giving gets twisted. *Twisted?* Yes, the simple act of giving can get turned around so that we lose the beauty of the blessings that God intended.

Our giving gets twisted when we "give to get." Remember, the blessings God gives come back like boomerangs. If we expect to get some sort of direct blessing back from our giving, we're going to be quickly disappointed. The street guy isn't going to buy you dinner if you buy him lunch. If you do an act of kindness for someone that you will never see again, that's it. If I have $35 in my pocket and I give the $35 away to sponsor a child, I now have nothing but lint in my pocket. You give it, and it's gone.

Another way that our giving can get twisted is when we give to get people to like us. If your motive for giving is to earn recognition and praise from people, watch out. That's going to come back to you like a boomerang too, but in a *bad* way. Jesus warned, "What sorrow awaits you who are praised by the crowds" (Luke 6:26). Trying to please the people is like a drug. It doesn't matter if it's one person or ten thousand. When they praise you, it feels really good in the moment, but it doesn't last. In order to get that feeling again, you have to try to please them again, and then again, and then again. . . . It's like an addiction, and you become a slave to it. It causes stress, it causes you to lose sight of God, it can open you up for abuse, and it can seriously lead you to compromise your values. No, the right way is a backward way. Jesus even said, "What blessings await you when people hate you and exclude you and mock you and curse you as evil because you follow the Son of Man" (Luke 6:22). That's weird, but that's right.

And finally, our giving can get really twisted when we do it to earn the approval of God. God's love for us never changes. He loves us because of what Jesus did, not because of what we do. He accepts us because Jesus died for us on the cross, not because we try to sacrifice ourselves for our cause. That's backward from the way we normally think. I think most of us believe if we give of ourselves and try to make a difference in this world, Jesus is going to pin a little badge on our vest at the monthly meeting and say, "Nice job. I'm very impressed. I guess I *have* to love you now." No, that's not it at all. God is crazy about you just the way you are. Our motives shouldn't be to *earn* God's love. (We already have that!) We are motivated *because* of God's love, and we give *because* of his love working through us.

Only one verse in the Bible says we should test God. It's Malachi 3:10 where God tells us to give, and then continues, saying, "Test me in this . . . and see if I will not throw open the floodgates of heaven and pour out so much blessing that you will not have room enough for it" (NIV).

The next time you feel "the nudge" to give, whether it's something huge or something as small as giving away a Coke, listen to what God is saying: *Do it. Test me. I dare you.*

Take Your Best Shot

In order to do something bigger than yourself in a way that is going to bless others as well as you, it's always a good idea to do an honest check of your motives. Find a place where you can spend some time talking with God. Read Psalm 139:23–24:

> Search me, O God, and know my heart;
> test me and know my anxious thoughts.
> Point out anything in me that offends you,
> and lead me along the path of everlasting life.

In what ways are you tempted to "give to get"? Write about the times you feel you did things to try to earn the approval of certain people or the love of God.

Ask God about these things, and he will show you. Pray that he leads you in the right direction.

Take Your Best Shot

Online: I love when things come back to me in ways I never expected. If you are moved by this book, or even just want to say hi, shoot me an e-mail at austin@hoopsofhope.org.

Take Action: Send out a boomerang blessing this week. Be creative, and plan a small blessing for a friend, family member, or teacher.

Chapter 7

Vision

"it is a terrible thing to see and have no vision. . . . the only thing worse than being blind is having sight but no vision."

{ helen keller }

I figure that John Larson has probably seen it all. He has been a news correspondent for a long time, and he has been to every poor corner of the world. He has seen war, and he has seen huge natural disasters. He was traveling with us in Africa when we asked him, "John, does anything you see ever get to you?" He stopped for a second and then said, "All that ever really gets me now is when I see that blank stare of a child. You can't really figure out what's going on, but it's this blank stare—an emptiness in their eyes. That gets me." I would soon find out what he meant, and what I saw would be engraved in my mind forever.

We had stopped at a regional office for World Vision. When I saw her, I saw the blank stare and the empty eyes that John spoke about. She was sitting on a concrete floor with both her arms wrapped around her brother's legs as tight as could be. Just sitting there, staring. It was almost like she was looking through us into the distance. I'm guessing that her brother was about twelve years old. She clung to him as if her life depended on him. What was she doing sitting on the office floor? Her brother had brought her there, hoping that she could get her picture taken, hoping that she might become a sponsor child.

She looked at me with the same look that I saw through the television screen the first day I saw Maggie. But this was different. Now I was experiencing it with all my senses. There was nothing separating me from her. She was there; I was there. Nothing insulated me from her reality. She and her brother sat desperately waiting for hope—and like all AIDS orphans, she had a name, and it was Abigail.

Blind, but Now I See

In order to take your best shot, in order to truly do something that's bigger than yourself, you need to be able to see differently. You need to be able to look at the world and observe things that some people don't even notice. You have to be able to see, and you have to have a vision. Vision is your *cause*. Vision is your *purpose*. Vision is your *heartbeat*. Vision is what you get when you see a *need* that captures your attention and have the *passion* to do what you love to do. Having your own vision opens you to God's possibilities. It blows the dust off of your dreams and highlights the fact that God wants to use you to make a difference.

I don't want you to finish this book and walk away with just a cool story. I want you to walk away with a burden on your heart. But not just any burden. I want you to be pursuing the purpose God has put on *your* heart—it has to be *your* vision. In fact, I'm a little bit worried that you might become a part of Hoops of Hope. Yes, you heard that right. *I'm a little bit worried that you might become a part of Hoops of Hope.* And it's because I want you to answer God's personal call for *you*. Honestly, I think it would be incredible if *everybody* did Hoops of Hope. I mean, if everybody joined in? Wow. It would be amazing. But my prayer for you is that God will give you your own vision of how you can take your best shot to make a difference in the world around you. Maybe that's through Hoops of Hope, and maybe it's something entirely new.

God isn't into cookie-cutter people. You know how cookie cutters work, right? You take that little metal star cookie cutter and press it into the dough over and over, and what do you get? A bunch of little stars that look exactly the same. But God made each of us unique. We don't all have five points, the same ingredients, and the same frosting. God isn't into that; God is into you.

How do you discover your vision? It happens when you see a need and when you discover your own personal passions. You have to have both. (If all you see are the needs, you'll get depressed! If all you have is passion, your life will be wasted on things that don't matter!)

Seeing the Needs

Okay, let me say this just one more time. If you get fired up about AIDS orphans in Africa and want to join Hoops of Hope or sponsor kids, that would be fantastic! But those certainly aren't the only needs on the planet. Our whole world is in need. If you keep first things first, and look at things like God does, he will show you the need that he wants you to be a part of.

For me, at the moment at least, my eyes are focused on the needs in Africa. After a quick online search of a couple of keywords, the statistics just jump out and grab me by the heart.

» 1.3 billion people worldwide live in poverty, living on less than one dollar per day.

» More than 26,000 children under the age of five die each day.

» Over 850 million people will go to bed hungry tonight.

» Every five seconds a child dies because of lack of food.

» Of the 11 million people in Zambia, 1.2 million are AIDS orphans.

» 60 percent of the people in Zambia are stunted in their growth because of malnutrition.

» The average life expectancy in Zambia is 41.

» Every 14 seconds another African child becomes an orphan because of AIDS.

» There are 15 million AIDS orphans worldwide; 12 million are in sub-Saharan Africa.

Those kinds of numbers are really hard to imagine. If 15 million children linked hands and stretched in a single line, they would reach from New York to Los Angeles and back *five and a half* times.

Let's make those numbers a little more manageable. Say a typical elementary school

15 million children would stretch from Los Angeles to New York and back again 5 1/2 times

has five hundred students in it. If six thousand children become AIDS orphans each day, that means the equivalent of all the kids in twelve elementary schools become orphans each and every day—they walk home to find out that one or more of their parents has died. . . . That I can imagine, and I don't like it.

The numbers are huge. But they aren't just numbers. They are people. These kids are just like you and me. They have dreams, they have a purpose, and God loves them just as much as he loves you and me. I believe that they should have the opportunity to pursue their dreams and to live out their God-given purposes. But they're not getting the chance to see their dreams come true because they are living in complete poverty.

Watching videos about the AIDS epidemic, corresponding with Ignatius, and researching Africa is how God made the need *really* real to me. The situation was so extreme. It wasn't like, *Oh, Austin, you have all this extra stuff in your life and you need to give some of it to them.* Our standards of living may never be in balance with everyone else. Someone is always going to have more, and someone is always going to have less. No, the goal is not to make things *equal*. The goal is to make things *livable*. These kids don't need my iPod. They don't need a cell phone or computer. They don't even need electricity (for thousands of years the whole world lived quite happily without it). It's not about downloads; it's about HIV (the virus that can kill). It's not about SUVs; it's about drugs called ARVs (which can keep an AIDS victim alive for years). It's not about PS3s; it's about CD4s testing machines (to help the doctors know what amount of drugs to give the patients). It's not a matter of having more or less; it's a matter of life or death. This is the need that has captured my heart.

Enough about me. What about you? Has God shown you the need that will become part of your vision? The place to start is to think about what touches your heart. What wrongs do you see in the world around you? What do you know could be better if *someone* would help? The possibilities are so endless, but if you need some inspiration and information, check out the Ministry Resource Guide on page 216.

Any place you find people, you will find needs. You'll find them in your own country, in your own city, in your own school, in your own class, or maybe even in your own family. Think about it. What about that person sitting alone at the back of the room? Or even closer than that, what are the needs in your own home?

A "need" doesn't have to be this massive global problem that will take a lifetime to conquer. Needs can be very small, very specific, and exist for just a moment or two. Some needs are physical—in places all over the world people need food, medicine, clothing, and shelter. Some needs are emotional and mental—people need an education, a smile, a hand to hold, a challenge to accomplish. Many needs are spiritual—there are millions and millions of people on the planet who don't even have a Bible in their own language. Many cultures don't have a single church. They don't have any way to find out about Jesus. That's a very big need indeed.

Needs are everywhere, and they come in every shape and size. That's why it's so important to make your relationship with God your number one priority. You never know when or where God is going to want to work through you to reach out to someone. Seeing the need means learning to see what God wants to show you, because he has something in mind for you to do—something bigger than yourself.

Discovering Your Passion

Seeing the need is one part of catching a vision. The

other part is discovering your passion. Finding your passion can be pretty easy. You just need to be honest with yourself and figure out what you really like to do. Sometimes other people expect us to do certain things or to play certain sports or get good grades or whatever. Sometimes we forget about what lights us up in our own hearts. I think the most brilliant question I've ever been asked is the one that Mr. Buck from World Vision asked me: *What do you like to do*? I'm certainly not as brilliant as Mr. Buck, but I would rephrase his question to really discover your passion. I would just add a little to it: *What do you like to do more than anything else*? You probably like to do lots of stuff, but it's the thing you like to do more than anything else that is your passion.

For me, that was a no-brainer. I like to play basketball. I love putting on my favorite pair of basketball shorts and going out to hit the court. It's just my thing. But I like other things too. I love hanging out with my family and watching movies. I like texting. I love Crunch Wrap Supremes from Taco Bell. And I like girls. But none of those things are my passion. If they were, I'm sure God could have used any one of them to help AIDS orphans . . . even Crunch Wrap Supremes!

The cool thing is that you don't even have to be good at what you like to do. You don't have to be a starter, you don't have to be the captain, and you don't have to be the soloist. You just have to be willing to use what you love to help with the need. Remember when I told you that I stink at basketball? When it comes to shooting free throws, I make about five out of ten from the line when I'm rested. (Imagine how bad I am after I have shot a couple hundred.)

You might be thinking to yourself, *I'm not good at anything.* I think everybody is probably pretty good at at least one thing. Think math, music, art, the Internet, chess, video games. Did I just say *video games*? Yes! God could even use video games to meet a need. But if you're convinced you stink at everything (like I stink at basketball), so what? Find what you like to do more than anything else, and you will find your passion.

Passion is essential for vision; it's the other half of the equation. Make it a goal to discover your passion. Ask God to keep opening your eyes to the needs around you. When the needs and your passion collide, you'll find your vision in the middle of the mess. It's like your heart and God's heart get all mixed up together. You'll get his eyes. You'll find your passion. You'll have vision.

Back on the Line

I didn't have that all figured out when I was ten, the first day I was shooting free throws in the school gym. It was just so simple at that point. I saw a need: AIDS orphans. I knew my passion: basketball. I think that's why everything felt so great on that day, because I was living out my vision. And it's a good thing, because I needed it—I was really starting to hurt. My mom and her friend were counting the free throws. About every 50 they would let me know how I was doing . . . 350 . . . 400 . . . 450 . . . By 500 it started to get really painful, and I still had a long way to go. Every once in a while, kids from the PE class would look over from the other side of the court and come help rebound or watch or cheer me on. One of my friends, Emily, rebounded for me a lot. Because I'm so terrible, she was running all over the gymnasium. (She should have gotten people to sponsor her for every time she chased down one of my bricks!) She was as tired as I was, but her encouragement was incredible. My grandma brought me some Chinese food for lunch. That helped.

The shots kept flying. By the time I hit 1,200 I didn't just hurt; I was numb. My dad's old friend, Kurt, called.

We prayed over the phone that God would give me the strength to make it. It meant the world to me. To have people supporting me? That was priceless. But none of this would have made sense if I hadn't had a vision. I kept on thinking about those kids—kids like Maggie and Ignatius. I knew that what God was doing in that gym was impacting kids half a world away. With every shot that went in the air I was thinking, *That's for one more child.* We've actually written down a Hoops of Hope "vision statement" that combines the needs we see with the passion of our hearts:

> To care for the 15 million children who have been orphaned by HIV/AIDS by allowing children, teens, and adults to participate in a fun, life-changing event.

It's been years since that day, but our vision statement is unchanged. In fact, I can see it even more clearly than ever before. Now, when I close my eyes, I can still see Abigail sitting on a concrete floor of the World Vision office, clinging to the leg of her brother. *Is she still alive? Is she still hoping that someone might see her picture at some concert and become her sponsor?*

❯ Taking His Best Shot:

Matthew

British Columbia, Canada

Sometimes, catching vision can cause you to do crazy things.

My friend and I were talking on the phone, and out of the blue she told me about Hoops of Hope. She offered to get me involved, and she e-mailed the Web site to me. I watched the video, and I thought the whole thing with AIDS in Africa was tragic. I wanted to do something about it. It took about five minutes to set up my account on the Web site. I shot the last two years—1,000 free throws each time. The first year it was about -1 degree Celsius (about 30 degrees Fahrenheit) and snowing really hard. We lasted for about seventy shots and then it got too cold, so we finished off the baskets at the school. I know that sounds crazy, but I also know that I was helping kids in Zambia, Africa. It was the best feeling ever! I loved the fact that I was making a difference in kids' lives, and I was helping by playing the sport I love.

God can use you to make a difference too. All you have to do is see the need and then apply your passion. But be careful, you might just end up shooting hoops in Canada in the middle of winter (not recommended).

Visions change and grow. Sometimes they only last a moment; sometimes they last a lifetime. Just because I did something yesterday doesn't mean I'm supposed to do the same thing today or keep doing it tomorrow. In all honesty, I have no idea how long God will keep the Hoops of Hope vision alive. I do know that someday it will end. That's okay with me. As long as I keep God number one, he will keep showing me needs, and I will keep discovering new passions. I believe that God continues to ignite our lives with vision again and again. We might head one direction only to have God steer us in another. Some things we try will probably "fail." So what?! That's all part of taking our best shot.

Maybe someday you'll be on the free-throw line with us. Maybe not. That doesn't matter. What does matter is that you find your own vision, and then keep on finding it. You need a vision statement of your own because everyone needs to care about something. We were created because we have something to offer. No matter where we are, no matter what our skills, and no matter what our age, we can make a difference. Don't let anyone tell you otherwise.

During an average human lifetime, the heart will beat 2.5 billion times. What is your heart beating for? What is your vision? What keeps you up at night? What would you do about it if you knew you couldn't fail? Answer that, then go out and do something about it with your passion.

Take Your Best Shot

Find a place to have some Quiet Time alone with God and read Matthew 25:31–40:

> But when the Son of Man comes in his glory, and all the angels with him, then he will sit upon his glorious throne. All the nations will be gathered in his presence, and he will separate the people as a shepherd separates the sheep from the goats. He will place the sheep at his right hand and the goats at his left.

Then the King will say to those on his right, "Come, you who are blessed by my Father, inherit the Kingdom prepared for you from the creation of the world. For I was hungry, and you fed me. I was thirsty, and you gave me a drink. I was a stranger, and you invited me into your home. I was naked, and you gave me clothing. I was sick, and you cared for me. I was in prison, and you visited me."

Then these righteous ones will reply, "Lord, when did we ever see you hungry and feed you? Or thirsty and give you something to drink? Or a stranger and show you hospitality? Or naked and give you clothing? When did we ever see you sick or in prison and visit you?"

And the King will say, "I tell you the truth, when you did it to one of the least of these my brothers and sisters, you were doing it to me!"

Ask God to open your eyes to see the needs that he wants you to see. Ask God to help you discover your passions. Write out a list of your passions. What do you like to do more than anything else?

Now write out the needs that grab your heart the most. What breaks your heart?

Can you combine these needs and your passions into a single vision statement? This may take some time, so don't worry about it if it's not clear to you at the moment, but you can start to brainstorm below.

Online: Go online and use the time you usually spend on things that "expire" to find out about an issue you care about. Some cool sites to check out:

Invisible Children: www.invisiblechildren.com
International Justice Mission: www.ijm.org

Don't forget to check out the Ministry Resource Guide on page 216 for information on these and other organizations.

Take Action: The most important thing you can ever do for anyone is to pray for them. Please spend some time praying for the people in Zambia. And keep asking God to show you your passions and where he'd like to work through you to help others.

Chapter 8

Supernatural Size It

"in this life we cannot do great things. we can
only do small things with great love."

{ mother teresa }

Why is it that everybody thinks bigger is better? You know, we all want to have the most friends on Facebook. We want to score the most points and get the best grades. Guys want the best six-pack abs and the hottest girlfriend. We hope that someday our picture and our name will be on the wall of the gym. Girls want . . . Hmmm, I guess I don't know what girls want. Oh well. For us guys, though, we want the biggest and the best.

But really, bigger isn't always better. God is not impressed with the world's version of big; yet, we have a God who knows how to supernatural size the smallest of things. This is one of my favorite stories:

Early one morning a boy was walking along a beach. Hundreds of starfish lay stranded on the shore, having been washed onto the sand the night before by a storm. As he walked, the little boy would pick up a starfish at random and throw it back into the sea. An old man came down the beach, walking in the other direction. He asked

the little boy what he was doing. "I'm saving star-fish," he answered. "Young man, don't waste your time. There's no way that you can make a differ-ence for all these starfish," the man said. The little boy leaned down, picked up one more, and threw it back into the sea. He looked the man in the eye and said, "I made a difference to that one."
—adapted from the story by Loren Eiseley

Who's the one on the beach waiting for you? Who's the starfish in your life that you need to help? You might think that you are just one person in this world. But to one person, you might be the world.

Never in my wildest dreams could I have imagined what was going to happen that day I started shooting hoops in the gym. My goal was to shoot 2,057 free throws, collect my pledges, and make a major difference in the lives of a couple of kids. It was going to be a one-day event. I was going to take my best shot at doing some-thing bigger than myself and that was it. My parents were going to take me out to our favorite burger place to celebrate and life would go back to normal. We had no other plans, no other agenda. But that's not the way the day turned out in the end.

When I took those first shots, it was just me and a handful of friends and family in the gym. Then we got a call from a local radio station. They interviewed me over the phone, and the story got blasted across the airwaves. That was really neat. Not long after that, a couple of local TV news crews showed up. (I guess there wasn't a lot of news going on that day.) It was cool, but there was one problem: my pants kept falling down. Picture it. I'm a skinny little ten-year-old, and when you're ten every free throw is a jump shot. You have to give it everything you've got just to make it to the rim. Every time I jumped up, my pants headed for the floor. I almost had to shoot with one hand so I could hold my pants up with the other. I was thinking, *Great, Austin, you're going to end up on TV, and the newscaster is going to announce, "Ten-year-old shoots air balls for AIDS victims with his pants down!"*

Then my class kept sending in people to check on me. "Hey, Austin! What number are you on?" That might not seem like a big deal to you, but it was to me. See, we had just moved to Arizona from Southern California. I was new to that class. And now I was doing this weird thing in the gym. I didn't think anybody would understand. When I realized that my class cared about me and what I was doing, well, that meant the world to me. (Still to this day, my school supports me a lot.)

Then more people started showing up. When I started to get close to two thousand, there were maybe sixty people in the gym. (That was about fifty-eight more than I had planned on.) They started counting down: "Fifty! Forty-nine! Forty-eight!" My heart just kept racing faster and faster. My arm was totally numb, but with all the encouragement, my second wind kicked in. "Twenty-five! Twenty-four! Twenty-three!" Every time I happened to make a basket, they cheered. I was like, *Wow! This is incredible!* When I got to five, the whole world went into slow motion. I could see the banner my mom and sister had made; I could see the ball; I could see the basket. I could see the faces of all those kids in the videos—each shot was for one of them. "Three! Two!" (Those were for Maggie and Ignatius.) And finally . . . "One!"

With all my might, I let that last ball fly. It felt incredible—like a Hail Mary touchdown pass at the end of my own private Super Bowl. Amazingly, the ball bounced off the backboard, off the rim, and then through the net. Everyone screamed, rushed over, and began hugging in one big mob. I had never had so much fun in my whole life. I had reached my goal. God had done something important through me. Now I was celebrating with family, old friends, and new friends. That alone was huge. That was plenty big for me. I couldn't imagine anything bigger. But by the end of that day, we had been on the news, someone sent us to the Suns game, and I even got to meet the NBA player, Steve Nash. Wow. What I thought was going to be a simple event turned out to be really big. That was a "supersized" day.

The thing is, I could have never made all of that happen. Not in a million years. That's why we have to be obedient to the small tasks God puts on our hearts and trust him to take care of the rest of the details.

Over and over, Jesus showed that it is the small things done in faith that matter to God. (See Mark 12:41–44.) For example, Jesus was in the Jewish temple one day, watching the rich as they gave. Then this lady came by, and she gave less than a penny. "She has given more than anyone else!" Jesus said, "because she has given all she had." And then there was the little boy with a few loaves of bread and a couple of fish. Jesus was teaching a group of about five thousand men, plus women and children, and they were starting to get really hungry. Andrew, one of the disciples, brought the kid to Jesus. He didn't have much, barely enough to feed one family. But Jesus took that little bit, and he thanked God for it. Then God supernatural sized it and fed the whole mob (see John 6:1–15.) Giving the small basket full of fish and bread was the boy's job. God chose to do a miracle and feed five thousand instead, but that was God's job, not the boy's. If Jesus had used the food to feed just one family, it would have been a total success—and it would have meant the world to that one family.

For some reason God takes great pleasure in small things. He also likes things that are done in secret:

> Give your gifts in private, and your Father, who sees everything, will reward you. —Matthew 6:4

> When you pray, go away by yourself, shut the door behind you, and pray to your Father in private. Then your Father, who sees everything, will reward you. —Matthew 6:6

If you *really* want to do something bigger than your-self, do small things and do secret things! It's one way to make sure your motives are in the right place, and you're keeping first things first. God rewards this! It's the boomerang blessings all over again. Maybe God will supernatural size it. Maybe he will use you to do things that everyone can see, but then again, maybe not. We just always have to remember, it's about his plan, not ours. I wasn't on the news that day so everyone could see how good-looking I am and what a great shot I have. (Trust me on this.) God put me there so that more people would know what's going on in Africa and how they can help. And even when doing his will and helping others doesn't involve TV crews and autographed jerseys, there's still nothing better. I really encourage you to start taking your best shot by doing small things and secret things. And then never stop doing them. It should be all about just you and God touching lives together. And it's really, really fun.

Along with doing small, secret things, I also believe it's time to dream God-sized dreams. I believe we are supposed to do *both*. Every Christian possesses a special ability to make a difference. And we have to trust that God can bless our efforts more than we could ever imagine, and he can give us the strength to do things we never could on our own. That's what faith is, but it's tough. In some ways I feel like I've lost a lot of my dream power. I'm afraid I'm starting to think more like an adult. I try to be sensible and reasonable. Sometimes I get concerned about the details. I think we all need to dream like we did when we were nine, back when nothing was impossible. Why? Because with God, all things *are* possible.

So what did you dream was possible when you were nine? If you can't remember, take a day and go hang out with some nine-year-olds. Ask them questions. Ask them what they want to do. Ask them about their dreams. Did you dream that you could fly? That you could be president? Check this out: How many of us wanted to be a doctor or a nurse or a policeman or a fireman or a teacher? When we were nine, we wanted to help people. We wanted to make a difference. That's the important part. We knew that back then. Everyone reading this book has the opportunity, and the responsibility, to make a difference. And please, don't wait, because the problems in this world aren't waiting. Besides, if you don't make it a habit now, when you're an adult, you'll think too much and be really busy with super boring things.

Do small, secret things. Dream big dreams. In order

to do something bigger than yourself, you don't have to change the world—you can just change the world for one person.

Take Your Best Shot

Take some time out and really ponder Matthew 6:1–4 and 19–21.

Watch out! Don't do your good deeds publicly, to be admired by others, for you will lose the reward from your Father in heaven. When you give to someone in need, don't do as the hypocrites do—blowing trumpets in the synagogues and streets to call attention to their acts of charity! I tell you the truth, they have received all the reward they will ever get. But when you give to someone in need, don't let your left hand know what your right hand is doing. Give your gifts in private, and your Father, who sees everything, will reward you. . . .

Don't store up treasures here on earth, where moths eat them and rust destroys them, and where thieves break in and steal. Store your treasures in heaven, where moths and rust cannot destroy, and thieves do not break in and steal. Wherever your treasure is, there the desires of your heart will also be.

Are you okay with doing good things without getting credit for them? Have you ever struggled with wanting attention or praise?

Why is God's way of doing things secretly, better? What does it make us realize?

Have you seen God supernatural size things in your life? When?

Online: Do something small for God today. Whether it's a private message of encouragement to one of your friends on Facebook or a nice e-mail to one of your parents, make someone's day.

Chapter 9

Team

"alone we can do so little; together
we can do so much."

{ helen keller }

Some jobs are not meant to be done alone. That's just common sense, but I had a major reminder of that truth my first night in Africa, the night we met that giant spider. After we all finally settled down and climbed onto our mattresses, we turned off the generator that kept the one light bulb in the office burning. It got dark. Really dark.

That's when I felt the urge. I just had to go to the bathroom. Bad, bad timing. I wasn't about to face the Chihuahua spider and his entire family alone, so my dad and I put on our headlamps and headed out. This was not like going to the bathroom back home. This bathroom was basically a slab of concrete with a hole in it surrounded by four walls and a small door . . . and it was outside, about seventy-five feet from the building where we were sleeping. The night was perfectly still. I thought I heard some rustling beside us. Was it the spider coming back with his buddies? No. Just my imagination.

We finally got to the "bathroom," and I made my dad

go inside first. I was right behind him when the narrow beam of his headlamp lit up a monster scorpion. He was huge! The shadow from our headlamps made him look even huger. The light scared him, and he started to run right at us. We backpedaled so fast trying to get out of there that my dad stepped on my foot and peeled my shoe right off. We were standing out there in the dark and I said, "Dad, Dad, my shoe is still in there! Go get it!" He looked at me like I was crazy and said, "Dude, we're in Africa. Nobody has shoes here. Be thankful you still have *one*."

All I can say is that I'm really glad I wasn't out there alone. That night I was glad I was with my dad because sometimes it's just best not to go by yourself. Sure, you can do certain things alone, but some jobs require a team—and making a difference is one of those jobs.

It was just like my dad to willingly get up and go with me that night. That's what he's done all along. From the first time I told him I wanted to help Maggie, he's been there supporting me. So have my mom and sister. My mom has worked behind the scenes for years to help us at Hoops of Hope. And my sister, she's the best. She's the most supportive person I know. And if you ever come to a Hoops of Hope event in our hometown, you'll find my sister shooting or helping out wherever she can.

Like I said, some things just require a team.

When Team Happens

"Team" happens whenever two or more people with a common vision link together to accomplish their goal. A team can do what no one individual person can accomplish alone. Teams are powerful, and they are absolutely essential if we truly want to take our best shot and do something bigger than ourselves. The nice thing about doing small things in secret is that no one can stop you from doing it all by yourself. If you're going to do something bigger, however, there's no way you can do it without a team. In the best situations, the individual members of the team work together as if they were one, almost like they share the same body. In fact, that's exactly what the Bible says:

> Just as our bodies have many parts and each part has a special function, so it is with Christ's body. We are many parts of one body, and we all belong to each other. —Romans 12:4–5

On a team, we become part of something bigger, something more powerful, something that can do things we simply cannot do alone. Yet it also means that we must begin to live for others, and not focus on ourselves. Tim Hansel, the founder of Summit Expedition and a great Christian author, writes:

> Every cell in the body is designed for every other cell. The whole purpose of each cell is to enable all the other cells to perform. The only cell that exists for itself is a cancer cell.[4]

Who wants to be known as a cancer cell in the body? Not me! God designed us to work together in unity to maximize our strengths and cover our weaknesses.

Teams can be found in many different shapes and styles. A family can be a team. A youth group can be a team. A club at school can be a team too. "Virtual" teams can often be found on the Internet with only a few mouse clicks. You and one other good friend can be a team as well—all it takes is two or more people working together to fulfill the same vision.

Taking His Best Shot:

Michael

South Dakota, United States of America

It all started when a group of girls from Michael's youth group decided to make a difference in their hometown. Their church had gone on a short-term mission project in some of the poorest parts of the country and to some of the roughest streets in large inner cities. The girls started asking why they had to go so far away from their home to help someone. As they prayed, God led them to a small, but needy neighborhood just on the other side of town. It wasn't far from where they lived, but racial prejudice in the small town separated it in a major way . . . it was right next to door, but it was like a different world.

Sometimes twenty or thirty people were living in the same house. Alcoholism was terrible there. Many of the children would hide in stairwells or under tables to avoid drunken abuse. If the kids made it to school at all, they had to do so on their own. Many would show up late, having eaten nothing, or maybe they'd had just pop and potato chips for breakfast.

The girls decided to start an after school club in the middle of the neighborhood—a place where children could come for a few hours of sanity in the middle of this violent and neglected existence. Some of those girls were really good at organizing things. Some of them just wanted to love and hug on these neglected kids. Others put together Bible lessons and games. I helped with all of those things. But because I was bigger and older, my main job on the team was to help control the kids and protect them from the neighborhood bullies and gang members who sometimes tried to interrupt the club.

Working as a team, offering their individual strengths and skills for a common vision, the after school club went on for two years, touching lives with love and hope in a very dark situation. Together, they accomplished what none of them could have done alone.

Everyone needs a team, and teams need all sorts of people who have different things to offer. In order to

find your place on the right team, you have to be honest about what you're good at and also what you're not
good at. God has made you good at something. Maybe you
are good at building stuff. Maybe you are a good writer or
speaker, or a decent athlete. Maybe you like to organize
things or fix things. Maybe you're just really good at listening to people, or helping out when things need to
get done. Maybe you're good at telling people the truth,
or maybe you are really generous with your time and
money.

I think I'm good at encouragement. To *encourage*
literally means "to give courage." I think that's my
most valuable contribution on any team. My basketball
team loved me on the bench. (And believe me, I spend
plenty of time there.) They say I'm the best cheerleader
ever because I'm really good at encouraging everyone.
That's really my whole goal for this book too. I'm hoping and praying that the Hoops of Hope story will give
you the courage to go out and make your own story.

Team Dreams

When I finally got home after that first day of shooting
2,057 hoops for Africa, I collapsed in my bed. It was

dark. It was quiet. Every ounce of my body ached. My brain was completely soaked with new experiences and thoughts. It had been an amazing day. Why? Because I was part of a team. God had pulled together my family, my school, and my friends. Some people gave money; some people gave encouragement. World Vision was a critical part of the team too. They were the ones who took the money we raised and put it to use helping children in Zambia. As I lay there on my bed, staring at the ceiling, I realized that this was more fun than anything I had ever experienced before. It was a different kind of fun. I never knew how fun it could be to do something meaningful like that with other people. Through a team, God had done something totally amazing. As I drifted off to sleep, an idea started swirling around in my tired brain: *What if the team got bigger? What if others got involved and did the same thing? What if a lot of people got involved? If I could get sponsored to raise this much money for the orphans in Africa, how much could we raise if lots of kids got sponsored?*

About a month later my mom and dad asked me, "Are you going to do it again?" I had been praying about it all quite a bit, but I hadn't shared with anyone what

I was thinking until that moment. "I think this would be more fun if a thousand friends did it next year," I said. They got a funny look on their faces—it was the same look they gave me when I told them I wanted to shoot six thousand free throws in a single day. They were like, "Okay . . . sure, bud. Yeah, we'll go out and do that."

There was just one problem. I could count the number of friends I had on one hand. But the idea got stuck in my head, and my mom and dad were willing to pray about it. We had just seen God do something amazing. Was it possible that he could do something even more amazing than that? We decided to give it a try. I started encouraging people. First I started talking with the few friends that I had, and I let them know that I thought this would be a whole lot more fun if we did it with a lot more people. Then I started to talk with people who weren't my close friends. That was a little bit scarier, but I just kept telling them that I knew they could make a difference in the world. I tried to give them courage by telling them I believed they could do it. People started spreading the word, and what happened was amazing.

When December 1 came around that next year, all

sorts of people joined us for Hoops of Hope. One person shot free throws on the other side of the country in Atlanta, Georgia, and another in Washington State participated. I had told my friends, and the word spread. In addition to those two kids, me and my friends, plus two churches here in Arizona, and my old friends in California had events. Even an eighteen-month-old shot hoops! He stood there tossing his ball into a Little Tykes hoop.

Me? I shot some hoops, but I also got to do what I do best. While other students were shooting their Hoops of Hope, I got to rebound for them; I got to help build them

This was a Hoops of Hope event at our home church in Arizona.

up when they were getting tired. I kept reminding them of why they were doing this, thanking them for being part of our team, and letting them know that they were doing something that would have an eternal impact. It was the best. By the end of the day, over a thousand kids had participated in six different locations across the country. Once again the media was part of the team as they spread the message about AIDS in Africa and what kids can do to make a difference. When the last basketball arced toward its hoop, the team had generated $38,000—enough to sponsor over a hundred AIDS orphans in Africa. One hundred Maggies and Ignatiuses.

Back at Home

I was shocked, but it shocked plenty of adults too. I think they realized kids *want* to make a difference and that kids *can* make a difference as long as they are part of a team. I was just kind of shaking my head thinking, *Man, how could it ever get better than that? How could we ever top that?* The answer, of course was, that we couldn't. We couldn't top anything, because we weren't doing it. It was always God. That day he showed us what he can accomplish when we all come together with a common vision and let him work through us. When I lay in bed that night, I had trouble sleeping again. Now that we had a team, it was time to dream again. *Yeah, it was great to help a hundred kids. But what if we did something really tangible? What if we built something? Something we could see, something huge that could touch the lives of thousands and thousands of kids in Africa?*

Dream On

If God can use us to sponsor over a hundred kids, what can't he do?! I started dreaming about what God might do next. This time I was getting the feeling that he wanted us to do something we could see, something that would touch thousands of AIDS orphans.

"I'm thinking about a hospital or a school," I told my mom and dad. "I think we should build something major that could help thousands of kids." My parents just laughed—but they weren't laughing at me—this time we were all laughing together. We had all seen what God had done over the last two years, and we were all starting to believe that the impossible was possible.

The more we thought about it, the more a school seemed to be the way to go. When someone becomes educated, they are empowered in every single way. Education is really the only way to fight the spread of HIV and AIDS. But where in the world do you start? You don't exactly go on eBay or craigslist and find a school in your price range. We did a ton of research and got discouraged because we couldn't find anything. But it turned out that God already had one picked out for us. One day Mr. Buck called from World Vision. He was so excited. "I've got something that I think is going to blow you away," he said. "There's a guy who worked for World Vision named Jonathan Sim—a passionate individual who loved God and had a huge heart for AIDS orphans. He recently passed away, and his wife, Kelly, wants to build a school in his honor in a little village called Twachiyanda in Zambia. Austin, why don't you join with Kelly and help her make Jonathan's legacy a reality?"

We were hooked! It seemed like the right project with the right people in the right place. And again we had to laugh; we were trying so hard to figure this out on our own and take control of it ourselves. God surprised us with something we had never thought of.

The word started to spread very quickly. We contacted the kids who had shot hoops the year before. E-mails started going out. People were sharing the vision with others. I was able to speak at a couple of churches, and people started saying, "Wow, something's going on here. Kids are making a difference, a *real* difference." Did everything go perfectly smooth? Of course not. In many ways, it was tough—lots of trials and sorrows, just like Jesus promised. That's just the way it is. But when World AIDS Awareness Day finally rolled around that third year, 1,500 kids in eleven states were shooting hoops for the school in that little village! By the end of the day, more than $85,000 had been raised!

One of my friends had signed up early, but then he broke his ankle. It didn't stop him. He shot one thousand free throws with a broken ankle. And then there was another kid, an eighteen-year-old from the East Coast. He has autism and can't speak. Loud noises bother him, so he went off by himself and shot five hundred free throws. Three men we know have set the record for taking the longest amount of time to shoot their free throws. We didn't think that they would finish. One was in his mid-fifties, another in his mid-sixties, and the third guy was almost seventy. But they did it.

God had done the impossible again. Thousands of kids were going to be able to go to school because some kids gave up a day and shot hoops. That was just amazing. Absolutely mind-boggling if you think about it. Kids, teens, and adults in America went out and shot free throws. Because of them, men with shovels and cement on the other side of the earth began to clear the way for the only high school in the whole region—a school that would educate thousands and thousands of kids, showing them how they, too, could be used to make a difference in their world forever. Seriously, can you believe that?! It was just so cool!

Something amazing happened when all those people came together for Hoops of Hope. I don't know how to really describe it, but something incredible and bigger than ourselves happened. If you've ever been a part of a team, you know what I'm talking about. When two or more people come together to fight for a common vision—for something that truly matters—it really does mean something; you can feel it.

No matter where we are, no matter what our specific vision might be, I think it's important that we stop and take a look around and try to soak in everything that is going on around us. Is "team" happening?

We all need one, and somewhere out there is a team that needs us. God wants to use you. He also wants to use all of us as part of something that is bigger than ourselves. When we work together, the possibilities are absolutely incredible. That should be enough to keep you awake at night dreaming about what kind of difference you can make in this world. It sure does that for me.

Our team had come together to do something bigger than ourselves. Because of them, my dad and I prepared to travel halfway across the world to see what God and our team had accomplished.

Take Your Best Shot

Being part of a team starts with the right attitude. Grab your Bible and find a quiet place where you and God can be alone together.

But our bodies have many parts, and God has put each part just where he wants it. How strange a body would be if it had only one part! Yes, there are many parts, but only one body. The eye can never say to the hand,

"I don't need you." The head can't say to the feet, "I don't need you." . . .

All of you together are Christ's body, and each of you is a part of it . —1 Corinthians 12:18–21, 27

What kind of teams or groups are you a part of?

How does being part of a team make you feel?

Listen to what God is telling you about his body and your place in it. How do you feel a part of God's team?

Take Action: If you and your team would like to host a Hoops of Hope event, it's easy! Check us out at www.hoopsofhope.org and click on the "Host an Event" link, or e-mail us at host@ hoopsofhope.org and send us the following info:

Take Your Best Shot

- Your name, contact number, and e-mail address

- Desired location of event (city, state, and gym if you have one)

- Are you affiliated with a team, school, or church?

- When would you like to host your Hoops of Hope event? (Choose one of the National Hoops of Hope dates, or choose your own date.)

- Expected number of participants

This will get you started!

Chapter 10

One Pink Soccer Ball

"if you can't feed a hundred people, then just feed one."

{ mother teresa }

On the Forgotten Continent

We had been in airports and airplanes for over twenty-four hours before the vast expanses of the African continent appeared beneath our airplane. I love flying. I love the excitement of going someplace new—and this place was definitely new. We were finally on our way to Africa, "the forgotten continent," to attend the grand opening of a new high school in Zambia, a high school built with money raised by Hoops of Hope.

In the capital city, Lusaka, we met with Bruce Wilkinson. He runs a relief organization called Rapids, which works to help people living with HIV/AIDS and children orphaned by AIDS. Bruce took some time out of his busy schedule to explain to us what was happening with AIDS, orphans, and the country. We were listening and nodding our heads, but I guess it was clear to Bruce that we didn't fully get it. Finally he stopped. He took a deep breath and looked us straight in the eyes. "Look, guys. I don't think you understand. We're not playing a game here. Every single day, someone from my office is going to a funeral for someone that they know. It's a real thing that is impacting thousands of people's lives daily."

It was one of those quiet moments you don't forget, when someone tells you the truth about yourself. Was it possible that I still didn't completely "get it"? I thought I saw the need; I believed I had discovered my passion. I thought this trip was going to be "the icing on the cake." Did I still need to go deeper? I was about to see the best and the worst of Africa.

Two-thirds of a Church

Another long and dusty road was taking us far from the capital city. I wasn't sure where I was, and I wasn't sure where I was going as the African plains continued to roll beneath the wheels of our Land Rover. We finally stopped at a simple concrete structure with a tin roof. Large rocks held the tin in place; the dry African air blew through holes in the walls, which had no windows or doors. Was it a warehouse? Maybe a large stable for animals? No, it was a church, a plain and basic building actually, but so very beautiful at the same time. The empty shell of the building was filled and overflowing in a way that I had never experienced before.

The sign on the church we visited in Zambia.

We were packed inside. The adults sat on logs. I squished in with the children who sat on the concrete floor. Everyone was excited to see us. Visitors are not common in that part of the country. But at the same time, I felt immediately at home. On the wall was a sign carved into a slab of concrete. It looked like it had been scraped out with a stick. It said, "Welcome to the House of the Lord." I was ten thousand miles from my house in Arizona, yet here, in this desolate area with total strangers, I felt like I was in my place. Exactly where I was supposed to be.

I cannot begin to describe the way worship flowed through that building. It was singing that celebrated, dancing that praised, voices and instruments that seemed to echo off of heaven itself. They had little shakers made from bottles with rocks in them and a few homemade guitars. With perfect pitch they sang. I got the goose bumps, and I could feel the hair standing up on my arms as the Tongan worship spread out across the plains.

When it was time to pray, their prayers were focused far away. They prayed about their brothers and sisters in Zimbabwe, a country that is as poor as Zambia, but is now being torn apart by war. I was stunned. Here they are living in a land destroyed by droughts and disease, and yet their concerns were for others? The prayers and the worship and the message all seemed so right, so pure, so perfect . . . but it wasn't.

At first I didn't even notice it. In a new and unfamiliar place, I guess you don't always notice something that's missing. But when I did, it sent shivers down my spine. Something was wrong, terribly wrong—almost creepy. The church was filled with tons of kids. Kids were everywhere, and there were grandparents too. I'm guessing there were about two hundred of us packed into that small space, but when I looked around, I finally realized who was missing. The parents simply

One Pink Soccer Ball

weren't there. It was like they had mysteriously evaporated. A whole generation was missing. I knew that there were 15 million AIDS orphans, but I don't think I could really believe it until I really saw it. This little church in the middle of nowhere was a snapshot of what was going on in the whole southern half of Africa. The lucky kids have a grandparent or a great-grandparent, but the rest? How did they survive? How did they live?

After the high of the church service, I felt my emotions crashing down. The immensity of the problem swept me away. *Millions and millions of starfish stranded on the beach*, I thought. It all seemed so huge, why even try? Is there anything anybody can do that would matter? It sure didn't seem like it. I felt overwhelmed and hopeless.

George

As the church service ended and the people began to leave the building, a woman ran up to one of the men on our team. Words were flying from her mouth as she pointed at his hat. It was a World Vision hat. As tears welled up in her eyes, she kept asking in the Tongan language, "Do you work for World Vision? Do you work

151

for World Vision?" The man nodded, and the woman disappeared into the crowd. A few minutes later, she came back holding her boy. She was just gleaming; she had the biggest smile. She had big, beautiful eyes that were streaming with tears. She pointed to the hat again, then she pointed to her son. Her boy was a World Vision sponsored child.

George was unlike any of the other kids in the church. At nine years old, he was taller, stronger, and healthier than kids who were much older than he. He had clothes that were very simple, but they actually fit. The shirt he was wearing still had creases in it, as if it were fresh from a box. In fact, it was. George had just had a birthday, and his new shirt was purchased by World Vision with money that had come from his sponsor family in Tacoma, Washington. George's mom couldn't stop crying as she talked about them.

While the adults kept chatting, George and I and a few kids got a soccer game going. We used the best ball we had left—a pink soccer ball that almost didn't make the trip.

The afternoon sun beat down on our faces as the sweat soaked our shirts and dripped off our hair. Bare feet pounded the dirt, shouts rang out in different languages, and we ran as fast as we could just to feel the wind.

This was soccer, Zambian style.

I'm guessing that it was at least 100 degrees Fahrenheit in the shade . . . and we were nowhere near the shade. You might say that the Zambian kids had the home-field advantage, but then again, I was the only one who had shoes. It was the most incredible game of soccer that I have ever played, and probably ever will. It's memorable for a lot of reasons, but mostly because of George.

When we got ready to leave the "field," everyone was waving at each other. George gave me a big hug, and I thought, *I just have to give something to this boy.*

"Hey, George," I said. "I want you to have this." His smile stretched from ear to ear as he took the pink soccer ball from my hands. I knew he was thankful, but I had no idea how much it meant to him. I was about to find out. When we called it a day, I gave George the pink ball, and we went our separate ways. I never expected to hear from him again.

The next day we were at a site far from the church where we had played soccer. I was in a group of people when George's mother made her way through the crowd and greeted me. She handed me a letter. It took me a while to figure out what was going on. What was she doing there? It must have been important. *She had*

walked twelve miles to hand me a single sheet of paper?
I unfolded it.

Finally, finally, I think I understood. God had shown me the immensity of the problem. And then he showed me one child, one child whose life had been changed. I had always experienced child sponsorship from *my* point of view. Child sponsorship was such an easy, simple, and cheap thing to do. It just didn't seem like that big a deal. It almost seemed like a hobby or something. Deep down inside, I was never really sure that it worked. I enjoyed sponsoring Ignatius from *my* point of view, but now, finally, I was seeing things from *his* point of view.

This was about something bigger than a soccer ball; this was something bigger than some family in Tacoma, Washington, shelling out a few bucks a month. This was George's *life*. Child sponsorship is his food, his clothes, and his future. That family in Tacoma will probably

The letter from George.

never meet George, but God is using them; he is using them to make a difference in this boy's life. George's mother—the person who cares about him more than anyone else on the earth—is so grateful and so thankful that she was willing to walk twelve miles through the searing African heat to give me a letter of thanks.

I just stood there, stunned, trying to let it all soak in, but I couldn't. A huge wave of blessing was being poured all over me. George's life had been completely transformed by World Vision, and mine was changed, right there and then, by a single act of giving.

I knew the hand of God had touched us. I knew it for certain, because if it had been up to us, it never would have happened. We almost didn't bring the pink soccer ball. I almost missed out on that wonderful moment. The ball was a leftover, and we weren't even sure if it would hold air or not. It seemed kind of strange to pack it in our bags when it really belonged in the garbage can. It was my mom who suggested we might as well take it. "You never know. Somebody might want it," she said. My dad shrugged his shoulders and tossed it into a suitcase. Only God knew what was in store for it.

Now when I go to a concert or a conference and the band makes a big push to sponsor a child, I look at it a lot differently. I know that this works. I've seen the children who are waiting, and I know the desperation in their eyes. I know they are hoping that someone will pick up the card with their picture on it. We throw these little cards around like they're just paper. They're not. They're real little kids like Ignatius, Abigail, and George.

Bruce Wilkinson was right when he said, "Look, guys. I don't think you understand. We're not playing a game here." Now I think I finally understand. This isn't a game. People live. People die. God uses people to make the difference.

Yes, George truly taught me what I thought I already knew. When we take our best shot, when we trust God to do something bigger than ourselves, *it really does matter*. You don't need to meet someone in person to leave a fingerprint on their life. You don't have to change the world; you change it for one person. Somewhere in the process, it changes you too.

Take Your Best Shot

Read this story Jesus taught in Luke 10:30–37:

"A Jewish man was traveling on a trip from Jerusalem to

Jericho, and he was attacked by bandits. They stripped
him of his clothes, beat him up, and left him half dead
beside the road.

"By chance a priest came along. But when he saw
the man lying there, he crossed to the other side of
the road and passed him by. A Temple assistant walked
over and looked at him lying there, but he also passed
by on the other side.

"Then a despised Samaritan came along, and when
he saw the man, he felt compassion for him. Going
over to him, the Samaritan soothed his wounds with
olive oil and wine and bandaged them. Then he put the
man on his own donkey and took him to an inn, where
he took care of him. The next day he handed the inn-
keeper two silver coins, telling him, 'Take care of this
man. If his bill runs higher than this, I'll pay you the
next time I'm here.'

"Now which of these three would you say was a
neighbor to the man who was attacked by bandits?"
Jesus asked.

The man replied, "The one who showed him mercy."

Then Jesus said, "Yes, now go and do the same."

Do you know who would take care of you if something happened

to your parents? A godparent or grandparent? An aunt or uncle?
A family friend?

What would happen if there were no one left? Do you think
someone like the Good Samaritan would come along to help?
Why would someone do that?

What do you take for granted? Are there things you think are
"junk" that might be valued by someone else?

Take Action: Do a clean sweep of your stuff, and see what
things you rarely use that might really bless others—clothes,
toys, sports equipment. Gather it up, and make a run to your
local church, Salvation Army, or Goodwill store.

Chapter 11

Reality Check

"everyone has the power of greatness.
not for fame, but greatness. because
greatness is determined by service."

{ dr. martin luther king, jr. }

S ometimes I forget. I spend a lot of my time living just a regular life, a lot of us do, and sometimes I forget what it's like in Africa. I even live in a really hot, dry climate, and I forget. I'm from Arizona, where we actually take pride in how hot it gets. We always say, "Yeah, but it's a dry heat."

I go to the refrigerator and get an ice cold drink; I take an extra-long shower; I go to the pantry and try to decide what I want for a snack. I do these things almost every day of my life, and I forget what it's like in Twachiyanda, Zambia. I forget that they pretty much live in a desert too, because they are in the middle of a fifteen-year drought. There is no air-conditioning to shelter them from the scorching heat. There is no refrigerator, no shower, and no pantry. Often there is no food or water at all.

In the Sinazongwe region, the Valley Tongas were forced into the hills when a dam was built to create Lake Kariba for irrigation. It is the largest man-made lake in Africa, but the hills are incredibly rocky, and it's tough to grow anything there. There are more than six thousand children living in this area who go to bed hungry every single night and face starvation almost every day.

> **Taking Her Best Shot:**

Buna

Kathmandu, Nepal

Some people get AIDS by making bad choices. Some people get AIDS by accident. In the worst cases, some people get AIDS by force. That's what happened to Buna. When she was just a young teenager in Nepal, she was sold into prostitution. According to the U.S. State Department about 800,000 people are forced into the sex trade and shipped to different countries each year. Several organizations estimate that 200,000 Nepali women work in brothels in India—and seventy percent of them have HIV and will likely get AIDS.[5]

Buna became the first known AIDS case in all of Nepal. She was thrown out onto the streets to live as an outcast. That's when a woman named Shanta found her and took her in. She nursed Buna back to health, and they began a long-standing friendship. Through prayer and care, Buna has not only survived a life with AIDS, but she is now a "house mom" at the Peace Rehabilitation Center (www.peacerehab.org) where she cares for other girls who become AIDS victims because of forced prostitution.

It is difficult and heartbreaking work, but Buna understands why it is so important; she has been there. She is committed to making a difference in the lives of girls who need her the most—all because Shanta made a difference in hers.

Reality check: When you take your best shot at doing something bigger than yourself, you will come up against some challenges. Making a difference will be hard work; you have to keep your eye on the ball. It's important to remember how fortunate we all are here in America. We are blessed, and that's why it is our responsibility to take our best shot at helping anyone in need. We also have to help each other along the way.

I love to encourage people; I love helping people see a vision; and I love giving them courage to make a difference in this world, because that makes such a positive difference for everybody. But the reality is that sometimes we get discouraged. Our courage and vision can get taken away from us. We need to remember that too. Jesus reminded his disciples of this so they would not be caught off guard when tough times came:

> I have told you all this so that you may have peace in me. Here on earth you will have many trials and sorrows. But take heart, because I have overcome the world. –John 16:33

Trials

Making a difference takes hard work. The whole Hoops of Hope idea looks so cool on a video or a newsclip. What the videos don't show are the hours and hours of work that go on behind the scenes. They don't show my mom getting up early every morning and working on the computer. They don't show my dad giving up every single day of his vacation time to make this happen. They don't show the thousands of volunteers who drive trucks, move hoops (which are not light), deliver food, and sweep the gymnasiums. If you want to do something bigger than yourself, I have to warn you, expect to be tired, to be worn out, and to have to do the work that nobody else sees or appreciates. Remember though, you're doing this for a reason that matters, and God will give you strength because he's in you.

If you want to make a difference, you can also expect to be made fun of. Persecution can come from the strangest places. Sometimes Hoops of Hope gets e-mails from people who are absolutely ticked off that we are trying to help out in Africa. "Why don't you take care of your front porch first? What about all the problems in America?" they'll actually say. Sometimes people get angry when they find out I'm a Christian. Hoops of Hope isn't a Christian organization. We team up with tons of secular organizations that share our vision to care for the 15 million AIDS orphans. But I can't separate my faith from my purpose either. I guess that irritates some people.

If we focus on what others think, it can throw us off track. If you make a difference in the world, some people will be impressed and they will like you more for it. But sometimes you have to go against the crowd in order to stay true to what God has called you to do.

I was at a conference in China where six hundred students from around the world were talking about the most serious crises in our world. At the end of my message, one student asked me how we could prevent the onslaught of AIDS. I took a deep breath. "Africa has its own problems because they are so poor," I said. "But in countries like China and the United States? The best way to stop the spread of AIDS is to keep yourself pure and wait until marriage." Man, you could have heard a pin drop in there. I just put my hands up like, "Hey, that's how I feel." Then one dude in the back of the room started clapping, and then a lot of people started clapping, but there were plenty of people in that auditorium who didn't like what I had to say.

It's time to stop worrying about what others think. We need to change lives. If some people reject us because of that, so be it. I wish we lived in a world where people didn't spend so much time challenging others' motives and just went out and did something. But that's not the case. If you want to make a difference in the long haul, you're going to have to be convinced that God accepts you and God loves you even if other people don't. That's just reality.

Sorrows

If you want to make a difference, you have to know that there's also going to be pain mixed in with your joy. The need God places on your heart might feel like more than your heart can handle. I wouldn't trade my experiences for anything, but seeing the people in Africa who are suffering and dying is unlike anything I've ever had to deal with before. There's nothing easy about taking your best shot with a big lump in your throat.

Sometimes sorrow can come from what's happening on the inside of you. My family calls it "punkiness." (Most people call it pride.) Punkiness starts whenever we take credit for what God is doing, and we start to think that we are pretty awesome because of it. When we get "punky," we also start judging other people—we start thinking about how much better we are than they are because of what we are doing. My family calls me on this immediately whenever they see it happening. When I get prideful, I go to my room, and I spend a lot of time with God. I tell him that I know it's wrong and thank him for forgiving me. I ask him to take the pride away and to replace it with something better. Pride could totally mess up Hoops of Hope. If you take all our efforts and mix in just a little punkiness, our ability to help kids could be destroyed. Wouldn't it be horrible if we let a little pride get in the way of making an eternal difference? Around our house, we constantly remind ourselves that *it's not about what you do, it's about who you are that matters* . . . and all of that is from God.

Sometimes making a difference can make you feel really lonely too, like nobody else understands you. When we were in Africa, we visited a particularly bleak village, filled with starving victims of AIDS. Afterward, we stopped by Victoria Falls, the highest and most spectacular waterfall on the planet. It's also a big tourist destination. I was talking with a tourist who had gone to Africa on a safari. She rode around in a Jeep taking pictures of lions chasing zebras and stuff. She stayed on a beautiful ranch and visited a tourist village that showed what the African culture was like. Based on her experience, she only had one view of Africa. When I tried to talk with her about what was really going on, she just didn't seem to get it. I tried to convince her of the horrible needs, but she didn't see it. I learned from this conversation that some people won't see things the way I see them, and that's okay. We all look out at the world from our own unique perspective and are moved by different things, and sometimes we close our eyes to the big problems because we're afraid.

Fear of failure is a sad thing too. Sometimes adults

want to protect us as kids; they are afraid we might fail. I'm really lucky, because I have people around me who aren't afraid to fail. They aren't afraid to encourage me to try big things—even though the whole thing might blow up in my face. The reality is that it's not always that way. Or another thing adults sometimes do is treat us with this little condescending tone that says, "Ahhh, isn't that cute? Nice effort." Sometimes people will doubt whether or not you can make a difference at all. Don't worry about it. Just go do something and prove them wrong.

Doubting God can also kill our vision. Making a

This is me and some of the children I met in Africa.

difference often requires walking by faith and trusting that God will provide for our physical and emotional needs. If we forget that, we will get worried and fearful. I think this is a daily battle. We need to constantly remember what Jesus said:

> Store your treasures in heaven, where moths and rust cannot destroy, and thieves do not break in and steal.... No one can serve two masters.... You cannot serve both God and money.... Your heavenly Father already knows all your needs. Seek the Kingdom of God above all else, and live righteously, and he will give you everything you need.
> —Matthew 6:20, 24, 32–33

So, sometimes I forget what it's like over there in Africa, what it's like for people who are desperate for food, water, and medicine. But then I remember. I remember the people, the desert around Twachiyanda, and the rocky soil in the mountains above Lake Kariba. I remember that if you're going to take your best shot, there will be trials and there will be sorrows.

And then I remember that one person can make a difference and that God can use us to do the impossible.

Take Your Best Shot

The book of 1 Peter was written to people who were trying to make a difference in the middle of some very serious trials and sorrows. It is a reality check. They don't pretend that everything is smooth and easy. As you read the following verses, think about your own difficulties you need God to help you overcome:

> Now, who will want to harm you if you are eager to do good? But even if you suffer for doing what is right, God will reward you for it. So don't worry or be afraid of their threats. Instead, you must worship Christ as Lord of your life. And if someone asks about your Christian hope, always be ready to explain it. —1 Peter 3:13–15

> So then, since Christ suffered physical pain, you must arm yourselves with the same attitude he had, and be ready to suffer, too. —1 Peter 4:1

> "God opposes the proud but favors the humble."
> So humble yourselves under the mighty power of God, and at the right time he will lift you up in honor. Give all your worries and cares to God, for he cares about you.

Stay alert! Watch out for your great enemy, the devil. He prowls around like a roaring lion, looking for someone to devour. Stand firm against him, and be strong in your faith. Remember that your Christian brothers and sisters all over the world are going through the same kind of suffering you are. —1 Peter 5:5–9

What do you worry about? What scares you? Write down everything you can think of.

Now say a prayer and hand it all over to God.

What things in life make you struggle with your faith? How has God helped you overcome these reality checks?

Online: Taking your best shot can be overwhelming. That's why it's important to have a support system that will help you believe in yourself. Guys, *Breakaway* is a great place to start (www.breakawaymag.com). And girls can check out the speakers of the Revolve Tour (www.revolvetour.com).

Chapter 12

Hope from Hoops

"we must accept finite disappointment,
but never lose infinite hope."

{ dr. martin luther king, jr. }

It's an amazing thing to see a dream become reality, to be able to touch it with your bare hands. As we drove into the village of Twachiyanda, I couldn't stop thinking about where we had come from and where we were going. A year and a half earlier, we had dreamed of building something tangible with Hoops of Hope, something we could see, something lasting, something that could touch the lives of thousands of children.

As our small caravan finally came to a stop and the dust settled, I saw that dream become a reality.

We arrived at the Jonathan Sim Legacy School. Between the red dirt and the blue sky stood the most magnificent building. You probably wouldn't even take a second look at it if you drove past it in America. Here, in this place, where there was so little, the single-story blue and white structure looked huge. At least it did to me—it wasn't so huge in its size, but it was huge because it was a symbol of hope. And from what was going on outside of that building, I could see that hundreds of people felt the same way.

I got out of the vehicle and stepped into a mammoth

The school dedication was an awesome celebration.

celebration. It was like an explosion of color and laughter. Everyone was dressed in their best and most vibrant clothes. The excitement of the crowd just drew me in. A woman took me by the hand and walked me over to Chief Chikanta, the head of Twachiyanda. We sat together on big green couches underneath a makeshift canopy, which had been made with tree limbs and a tarp. I sat down with the chief, and we were surrounded by tons of government people who had come from all over the country.

They danced for the longest time, and I danced too. It was like their whole bodies were giving thanks for what was beginning that day. Minute by minute, I got a deeper glimpse into what this meant to the community. The chief spoke to the whole group, sharing his philosophy on the importance of education and how badly they needed it. "Education is the key to *everything*," he said.

When it comes to AIDS and HIV, the chief said that people just don't understand what it is. Once people know how the disease is transmitted, they know how to protect themselves and the people they love. In the new high school, two full sections of the curriculum would be focused on AIDS prevention and treatment. The topic is so important that it is treated like math, grammar, and science. Hundreds of students each year will learn about it, and they will also learn how to share the truth about AIDS with others.

The chief also told us how in Zambia a high school diploma gives you the possibility of going to college. That's huge. Most students only go to primary and elementary school. When they are done, there's really nothing for them to do except try to survive by farming for their families—and the fifteen years of serious drought have made that extremely difficult. Where there is no rain, there is nothing to farm. A high school diploma opens up the possibility of going to college and making a difference. When Zambians go to college, their goal is not to get a job so they can buy a nice house and cool cars and fun stuff. They send the money back to the village. The income from one or two college graduates can make a very big difference for the entire village.

This is the chief's biggest hope—that the people of Twachiyanda will break the terrible cycles of poverty and of AIDS. On top of that, the school will also have housing for orphans. Instead of living in abandoned huts or trying to survive in the open, they will have a safe place to eat, study, and sleep. "I have never seen such a gift coming from a young boy," he said. "Even though we knew his age, we were surprised at how small he was. This will go a very long, long way."

Many of the other government officials spoke as well. They said a lot about Jonathan Sim since the school was named in his honor. They talked about what a difference his family had made by sponsoring a child in that region, and what a beautiful gift it was from his wife, Kelly, to leave something like the school as a legacy in her husband's memory.

When the chief finally cut the ribbon as part of the

official opening of the school, there were so many people packed around that I couldn't see what was going on. I felt so small, yet I felt I was part of something that was so big. It was just amazing. I couldn't believe I was standing on the other side of the world taking part in a massive celebration because of what a bunch of kids had done in gymnasiums halfway across the globe. It just didn't seem possible. Finally, the chief asked me, "Why don't you show us how you raised money to build this school?"

We walked outside to a courtyard right next to the school. And there it was, the first hoop in the *entire* region. No one had ever seen or played basketball before, and in all honesty, it was clear that no one had ever built a basketball court before either! The posts were really crooked. The rim was sagging, and the court itself was seriously slanting. But let me tell you, that was the most beautiful basketball hoop I've ever seen. It was a real hoop of hope. It was a powerful symbol of everything that God had done.

The court was roped off, but the crowd surrounded it. Shoulder to shoulder, people were gathered round. I didn't realize how many people were at that dedication until I looked all around me. Some people had climbed trees; others tried to make their way through the crowd to get a better look. I felt like I was in a human coliseum.

They handed me a ball. I was thinking, *There's just no way I'm going to make it.* My dad pulled me aside and said, "Hey, bud, no pressure, but just so you know, the rim is about six inches too high, the wind is blowing so hard that the ball is going to blow about five or six inches in whatever direction the wind goes, and that's a pretty bad slope. By the way, the entire world is watching, but no pressure. . . ."

Great. But what could I do? I stepped into the open area between the wall of people, and I took my best shot. The first one missed, of course. I put the second shot up and it didn't look too good, but amazingly, it went in! The crowd cheered like crazy. I'm sure they were thinking, *What? This kid raised enough money to build a high school by doing this?!*

Who would have ever dreamed that one kid, one video, a basketball, and a hoop in America could be used to change lives half a world away?

Not me.

I never would have dreamed that. But I was watching a dream bigger than anything I could have ever imagined take place right in front of my eyes. I couldn't deny it. I was in Africa. I was able to see what God had accomplished. I was able to touch the hands of those whose lives have been changed by people thousands and thousands of miles away. I was able to hear the songs and watch the dancing as they celebrated a future that now had hope because some kids on the other side of the world had shot a bunch of free throws. It was an amazing day. It was a day that proved *anyone* can make a difference. It was a miracle. A total miracle. Something only God could do using a team of people who believed in miracles too.

The memories of what happened there will always be with me. But something else happened during that day that I will take with me forever. After everyone was done talking about the school, the chief got up again to speak. He said that when their village receives a gift from someone, they are called to give something back. What did he want to give me? He wanted to give me a new name. A Tongan name, the name *Maiya*. I was being adopted into their tribe as if I had always belonged. What it meant was that from that day forward, I was one of them. Then he explained that the name *Maiya* means "one who is quick to lend aid, and one who will tell our story."

A Calling

I do believe that it is better to give than to receive. But that day, I received so much that I just can't believe I gave enough to deserve it. In fact, I know that I didn't. I'll never be able to express what it was like to touch the hands of the kids we'd been trying to help. I'll never forget the adventure and the overwhelming sense of satisfaction after seeing our vision fully realized on the other side of the world. Sure, they were getting a school, but what I got? You can only get that by giving. That day I was able to see it, to hear it, to taste it, and to touch it. In the middle of AIDS hell, I was living heaven on earth.

I was allowed to experience some things that most of us will only experience after we die and are in heaven. I don't know why I have gotten to experience it here on earth. It might have something to do with the name that the people of Twachiyanda gave me. I'm called to try and be that person—the person who will tell their story.

Take Your Best Shot

I truly hope you've been spending intimate time with God at the end of each one of these chapters. Remember to always keep first things first as you discover what God has laid on your heart!

The apostle Paul prayed a powerful prayer for his friends in Ephesus in Ephesians 3:14–21:

> When I think of all this, I fall to my knees and pray to the Father, the Creator of everything in heaven and on earth. I pray that from his glorious, unlimited resources he will empower you with inner strength through his Spirit. Then Christ will make his home in your hearts as you trust in him. Your roots will grow down into God's love and keep you strong. And may you have the power to understand, as all God's people should, how wide, how long, how high, and how deep his love is. May you experience the love of Christ, though it is too great to understand fully. Then you will be made complete with all the fullness of life and power that comes from God.
>
> Now all glory to God, who is able, through his mighty power at work within us, to accomplish infinitely more than we might ask or think. Glory to him in the church and in Christ Jesus through all generations forever and ever! Amen.

That's my prayer for each of us too! Spend some time talking with God about that passage. Really listen to what he is showing you about who he is and who he can be in your life.

How do you feel after you spend time with God?

Has God ever laid a truth on your heart that you couldn't ignore? Or called upon you to do something for the kingdom? What was it?

Online: If you go to www.hoopsofhope.org and check out our You-Tube link (via the Follow tab), you'll get to see all sorts of videos that have helped tell the story of the orphans in Zambia. If you just search "Zambia," you'll see how many other organizations have been called to support the same cause.

Take Action: Want to have some fun with your friends? Produce and star in your own video to support your favorite cause. Post it online and spread the word.

Chapter 13

Contagious

"catch on fire with enthusiasm and people
will come for miles to watch you burn."

{ john wesley }

On December 19, 2007, at a Starbucks drive-through in upstate Washington, a customer decided that she didn't want to pay for her own drink only, but also for the car behind her, to wish the next person a Merry Christmas. It was a totally random and spontaneous act of kindness. The driver of the car behind her was shocked by this gesture and decided to pay for the car behind him. And this went on for 1,112 cars! Why? Because making a difference is contagious.[6] I know you're wondering who was in car 1,113 who took their drink and left, but that's not the point.

The word *contagious* means that something can get passed on from one person to another by direct or indirect contact. If you see a need, discover your passion, and pursue your vision, there's a good chance that others will follow your lead and go out and make a difference too. They do it because making a difference is contagious.

I was totally blown away by that day at the high school. It happened because a simple idea was passed from one person to another, and together we were able to do the unthinkable. But it didn't stop there. The guy who is in charge of education for all of Zambia heard about what had happened. He came out to see the school, and he was so inspired that he made a commitment to build an addition to the school, to put in solar power for a science lab, and to expand the housing for teachers. It's going to be a pretty awesome place when it's done—one of the best in the whole country. When you do something to make a difference, other people are going to follow.

This is what's happening out there. Kids, and adults, are finally seeing that they can make a difference—no matter what age they are. You don't have to wait until you're an adult. The fun and passion behind making a difference is catching, and it spreads from person to person. I am truly blown away by what God did to build that school, but at the same time it's hard to be proud of what we have done when you go to Africa and see how much more there is to do.

The Next Step

It looked like just another hut. Perhaps a little bit smaller than most, but really it was just one of thousands that we passed on our journey through Africa. I was learning, however, that each hut told a story—a story of real lives and real people, each one as important as you or me. We stopped at the hut, and the story was told. Eight children lived in this hut with a man. Their eyes were wide and their smiles were broad, but it was hard to look past their tattered clothes and the dirt caked on their shoeless feet. We were looking at the work of AIDS. The man was caring for several children who had been orphaned by AIDS. His wife had died of AIDS. His daughter had died of AIDS.

The dad was holding one of the eight children, his daughter—a little girl who was four or five years old, but who looked like she was two because she was so small. She had the eyes—empty eyes filled with sorrow and the distant stare that looks right through you. She had flies crawling all over her, going up into her nose and her ears. She was too weak to bat the flies away because she, too, had AIDS—and so did the dad.

It was almost more than I could handle. I had to force myself to go talk to this man. I just wanted the whole scene to disappear. I wanted so badly to turn away and go home. I had seen these images on TV, but now I was inside the TV, living it. The same questions haunted me over and over: *What if this were me? Why isn't this me?* Maybe I would have felt better if that family was unusual, but they weren't. It was normal life for millions and millions of people in the region; it was the story in almost every hut. Was there hope anywhere? Yes, there was. It didn't seem like much but when I looked again, I could see a glimmer of hope. In this terrible situation, "hope" was spelled A-R-V.

ARVs are antiretroviral drugs. They help people who have AIDS. They can't stop a person from dying, but they can help a person live a longer, healthier life. This

Here I am talking to the man with AIDs. The left photo is the old hut he and his family used to live in.

man and his family were lucky. He was taking ARVs; he could still care for the kids, and he had been able to build a little hut. (It wasn't big, but he was proud of it.) As a farmer, he was able to keep them fed with simple meals. He couldn't provide much, but he kept eight children from having to survive on their own.

That one man, taking that one simple drug, was helping to stop the vicious cycle of AIDS in his family and in his community. You see, the AIDS epidemic is not a simple problem. The disease, food, income, families, and entire community are interconnected. When a parent dies, it's not just that the child is left as an orphan. It sends a wave of devastation through the whole community. But when parents live, even for just a few extra years, they can continue to farm and provide food. They can still contribute and help out in the community, and, like this man, they can help parent children who otherwise would wander the streets trying to survive. I wondered, *Where would these kids go if this man was no longer alive?*

I was so excited that the school would help thousands of children. But then I thought, *If we can help thousands of parents, it could make a difference for tens of thousands of children.* A visit to a local hospital confirmed in my heart that a great opportunity was waiting. The "hospital" itself is really nothing more than a couple of broken-down rooms with almost no supplies. The tiny delivery room for new babies is also the AIDS testing center. In the blistering desert heat, people sat on the steps holding their children, just hoping to get in. It was unbelievable. Thousands of people in the area are infected with HIV, but only a handful of samples can be sent out each month to see if someone has developed into the AIDS stage. Then it takes a few months to get the results back. If they have AIDS, they must then walk thirty miles to receive treatment and ARVs. Most of them never make it. The vast majority never get tested, and those who do usually die before they can get the drug. *Could shooting hoops bring hope to this hopelessness?*

World Vision and the local staff of the hospital had an idea. What if we built a medical testing lab that allowed people to get tested, diagnosed, and prescribed with ARVs all in one day? The lives of hundreds and hundreds of parents could be saved every month. It would bring hope and hold families together. If we could keep the parents alive longer, the results would be incredible. Dads and moms could provide for their families for two more years, maybe more, and care for their kids through their teenage years. It would be a total boost for the entire community. It wouldn't be a cure, but it would help so much. But that wasn't all. World Vision's plan was for more than caring for physical needs; the labs would have counseling centers too. While doctors cared for the physical bodies, trained counselors would care for the souls, sharing with them the hope of Jesus Christ and eternity. What an amazing possibility.

The head nurse at the center was a big lady with a big accent, and she had a white outfit on with a big, white nurse cap on her head. She had heard about the new school, and when it clicked and she realized who I was, she was like, "Oh, oh, oh!" She started crying and hugging me and then cried and hugged me some more. They showed us around the little hospital, and then she showed me the ground where the medical testing lab would be built. (They were already talking like this was going to happen!) She was so excited. Me? Aside from being nearly suffocated by her hugs, I was feeling really overwhelmed.

I felt a huge burden as we walked away. I kept thinking, *Man I hope we can get this done. I hope we didn't promise something we can't deliver, because these people are desperate*. That's a huge burden to walk away with, especially as a thirteen-year-old. *These people are counting on us.* I knew about medical testing labs before that visit, but I didn't feel any sort of rush. If we didn't complete the next project that year, I thought it would be no big problem. Maybe we would just complete it the following year, kind of like when it was convenient for us—whenever we got around to it. But after seeing the man in the hut and visiting the hospital, I knew that if we didn't get the testing lab built, people were going to die. It was a blast of reality and responsibility that I had never felt before. *This is the real thing. It really matters. It's life or death.* As usual, we started to pray and trust that somehow God would work it out. I felt tremendous relief when I realized that if this were going to happen, it wasn't going to happen because of me; it was going to happen because God would do it through many people.

The next day we heard that people from the village had brought sand and rocks to the site of the future lab. It was a symbol of the hope they had. The hope that a bunch of kids around the world shooting baskets would someday save the lives of their families and friends.

Contagious or Crazy?

We returned to America with very mixed emotions. When you get the chance to see other places, you see how fortunate we really are. We were excited about what had been done, but seriously intense about what was left to do. Our family started by having this massive garage sale. We went through the whole house and cleaned out all the stuff we didn't need, sold it, and gave the money to Hoops of Hope.

But this was going to take a lot more than a garage sale. We were really depending on God for guidance and provision. Selling a bunch of our stuff is one thing; but building a complete medical facility on the other side of the world? We stood on the edge of the impossible again, wondering what was going to happen. God seemed to be moving, though. Kids, teens, and even adults started signing up for events again, and the word started to spread about the new needs. And then it *really* started to spread.

Teams from CBS and NBC had come with us on the trip to Africa. Their lives were changed by what they saw too. The story aired on the *Today Show* toward the end of November. While we slept in Arizona, the story was airing on the East Coast. The response was so over-whelming that our Web site actually crashed. As the show was broadcast across the different time zones, the message started touching lives, and then touching more lives, and then more. By the end of the year, ten thousand people from eleven different countries had shot hoops for the medical testing lab in Zambia. In April, CBS aired the story half an hour before the tip-off of the Final Four basketball tournament. About 11 million people saw it. Our Web site got 100,000 hits in less than ninety minutes. It was great exposure, but the question still remained: *Would people catch the vision and be willing to do something about it*? We knew, as usual, that only God could do that.

He did.

We needed $150,000, but in the end, over $200,000 came in. In the spring of 2009, I had the privilege of going back to Zambia a second time to dedicate the clinic. While we were there, we asked the head of World Vision over there how many people this clinic would help . . . one thousand or maybe even five thousand? He told us this clinic would save an entire generation.

By the time I got home from that second trip to Africa, Hoops of Hope reached full-funding for a second medical clinic. Not only had we funded one clinic, but now two clinics will help save even more people. Thanks to all of our exposure from the media, our friends and relatives telling everyone by word of mouth, and my involvement on the Revolve Tour, incredibly, twenty thousand people from seventeen countries shot hoops, raising $400,000. This lab will open in 2010, right next to the Jonathan Sim Legacy School. To be honest with you, I don't think anybody will ever know how many lives are going to be saved because people shot free throws. Yeah, making a difference is contagious, and making a difference can save lives.

Because we had some extra money from the building of the first clinic, we felt like God wanted us to make a difference for those who are dying too.

Love on Two Wheels

There's a huge grassroots movement going on in Zambia with regular people—regular people who are like angels to those who are dying of AIDS. They call them "caregivers." Caregivers travel from hut to hut to hut and basically just love on people as they are dying. I have

met them, and I think they are the most amazing people on earth. In the most difficult, dark, and demanding
hours of a person's life, they stand by them. They care
for their kids. They fetch their water. They prepare
their food. They pray with them and share the promise
of God's forgiveness and the hope of eternity. And when
these people breathe their last, the caregivers help
prepare the body for burial, make arrangements for the
funerals, and then help the families lay the body to
rest in the ground.

It is difficult, painful, and demanding work. But it
means so much, and it's so important that it almost
takes your breath away to imagine that they do this day
after day after day. World Vision saw what these caregivers were doing. They decided to try to help the
caregivers who were trying to help others. They
designed what they call "caregiver kits." Just a little
bigger than a lunchbox, they contain soothing oint-
ments to be massaged into the skin, anti-diarrhea
medicines, painkillers, washcloths, and soap. They
don't look like much, but in the hands of the caregiver, they are powerful tools of comfort and care for
the final days of life. Where did Hoops of Hope come in?
We teamed up with World Vision and World Bicycle

Relief to provide a thousand caregivers with kits and two hundred fifty bicycles that will help them as they travel from hut to hut.

Is there any way to explain this? I mean seriously, is there any logical explanation for why all this has happened? If Hoops of Hope were some massive organization, with all sorts of marketing dollars and big-time executives pushing a long-term strategy, then maybe we could say, "Yeah, we did that." But we can't. We are a family and a few friends and a couple of laptops working out of our garage and the spare room in the house. The only logical explanation is that making a difference is contagious. Thousands of volunteers and participants have been infected with the vision and are doing something about it.

Is it truly possible to take your best shot and do something bigger than yourself? Absolutely. The Bible says it's true, and all around the world people are stepping out to make a difference and proving it. We really are all part of the same contagious movement that was started by God when he loved the world so much that he gave his only Son, Jesus. Jesus made a difference. Then he chose twelve ordinary people to do something bigger than themselves and make a difference in the whole world. Now he is making a difference through *us*. He is showing us what he wants us to see. He is helping us discover the passions that he wants us to use. He is living through us to fulfill the vision that he has given us; a vision to go out and make a difference and spread hope. Yeah, making a difference is contagious. And isn't that the way it should be? After all, if AIDS is contagious and brings death, shouldn't hope be contagious and bring life?

Thank You

There are so many of you out there who have caught the vision. The story of Africa is one of great need, and I pray this book has told that story well and has shown you that you are not "expired milk" and that you have an incredible opportunity to truly make a difference for things that will last forever. But there's something else that I believe I need to tell you from my friends in Zambia, because their story isn't just about needs; their story is about gratefulness. I believe that they want you to hear them say, "Thank you."

For those of you who have shot hoops or helped with events, they thank you for the hope that you have brought to Zambia. The children, the tribal leaders, the dignitaries, they are saying thank you. And as far as that school goes? I personally want to thank you on behalf of the future generations of that region, and the thousands of lives that will continue to be touched through that building. For those of you who have sponsored children, I have seen the smiles on their faces, and I have seen the tears of the mothers whose children now have a future. They are saying thank you.

Some of you have never been a part of Hoops of Hope and never will be. You need to know that the world is full of people who want to say thank you for seeing their needs, discovering your own passion, and pursuing your own vision to make a difference. Thank you for letting Christ work through you; thank you for letting him love through you; thank you for letting him touch them through your hands. I have seen the people you are touching. I'm telling you what I know they want you to hear; they are saying thank you. They thank you, I thank you, and someday God will thank you too.

A massive celebration is going to take place in heaven. It will be a party and worship service like no other. A huge sea of people from every tribe, every tongue, and every nation will be standing before God in a huge celebration of worship. Everyone will finally be together—the *whole* team—and we will be raising our voices singing thank you to God, because he's the one who is responsible for everything and everything and everything.

Until then, keep the faith. Keep the focus. Keep first things first. We are a part of something bigger and more important than we could ever even dream about. And one day, all those dreams will become real.

Take Your Best Shot

In the very last book of the Bible, God describes a future worship service that is truly out of this world. He uses amazing word pictures and some stunning symbols to describe what is going to happen. Read these passages from Revelation 4 and talk to God about what you see:

> Then as I looked, I saw a door standing open in heaven, and the same voice I had heard before spoke to me like a trumpet blast. The voice said, "Come up here,

and I will show you what must happen after this." And instantly I was in the Spirit, and I saw a throne in heaven and someone sitting on it. The one sitting on the throne was as brilliant as gemstones—like jasper and carnelian. And the glow of an emerald circled his throne like a rainbow. . . . And they lay their crowns before the throne and say, "You are worthy, O Lord our God, to receive glory and honor and power. For you created all things, and they exist because you created what you pleased." —vv. 1–3, 10b–11

What's the best party or celebration you've ever been to? What made it so special?

What would it be like to be a part of this worship service in heaven?

In this passage, what was the focus of everyone's hearts? Who was getting credit for the amazing things that had happened? Write your thoughts below.

Online: What would happen if we could spread the message of hope faster than the HIV virus? Amazing things, that's what. Get online and use your God-given voice to start spreading the word. Use everything you can: blogs, Facebook notes, YouTube comments, forum posts, widget sharing, even a good old-fashioned e-mail! Talk about issues you care about, dreams and visions you have, books and Web sites that have inspired you, and find people who share your passion. Who knows what might happen. . . .

Chapter 14

Take Your Best Shot

"in the end, it's not the years in your life that count. it's the life in your years."

{ abraham lincoln }

God wants to use you.

I believed that back in the Introduction, and I believe that now more than ever before. I believe it for myself, and I believe it for you. If you walk away with one thing from this book, I pray that you've realized that *God wants to make a difference through you in a world that desperately needs you.*

Why? Because we are inheriting a world in great need. One day we will be the presidents, the pastors, and the missionaries of the next generation. Slowly our generation will be taking over. It's not a matter of *if* we will take responsibility; it's only a matter of *when.* Sooner or later, the world will count on us to make a difference. I think the sooner the better. Not only am I convinced that God wants to use you and use me, but I am convinced that he wants to use us *now.* The author Steve Farrar said, "Life is the only race you'll run where you don't know where the finish line is." You might have years left, or maybe just minutes. Remember, the only time God can use you is right here, right now.

God uses us when we see the needs around us,

discover our own personal passions, and capture a personal vision that gives life purpose and focus. When we put him first, there's no end to what he can do.

It's all a miracle, really, and I pray that you see the miracle of an awesome God using something like one pink soccer ball (or a basketball and a hoop) to unleash the power of hope in a dark and needy world. I pray that you see the miracle happen each day as God uses you—just as you are and just where you are—to make an eternal difference in this world. Yes, with God, all things are truly possible.

We've seen God use hundreds and thousands of ordinary people to have an eternal impact for those people in desperate need. I believe it's time for all of us, no matter what our age, to dream again of the things that are impossible. And when I say dream, I mean dream like you did when you were nine. Quite often people ask me, "Where do you see Hoops of Hope in five or ten years?" In all honesty, I don't have a clue. Five years ago, I *never* would have guessed that God would do what he has done. No way, not even close. If we had planned this ourselves, it would look so different. What's our strategy for the future? It's pretty simple. Our plan is to show up every day. As long as there's a need, we're going to show up until God tells us otherwise. That should be your strategy too! Don't worry about figuring everything out. Just keep God first, keep your eyes open for the needs he will show you, and do what you are passionate about to make a difference.

God is creating world-changers from our generation in every corner of the globe. I've introduced you to just a couple of them: Ayla, the girl with cancer; the orphans in Nigeria. These are just a couple of snapshots of the massive movement of young people who are rising up and taking advantage of opportunities to touch lives today—and you can add your name to this list, because God is going to use you too.

Can one person really make a difference? Absolutely. If you *still* don't believe me, let me introduce you to one more person who is making a difference in her world. She was born and raised in a country that has been ravished by AIDS and famine. Many would have considered her situation hopeless. No one would have blamed her if she grew up feeling like a victim of tough circumstances. But she didn't. Today, she is a world-changer in her own right.

> **Taking Her Best Shot:**

Maggie
Zambia, Africa

Do you remember the video that started everything? My "Maggie Moment"? Well, I wasn't the only one who saw that video. A woman named Betsy saw it too. She was touched by the desperateness of Maggie's situation. She saw that her great-grandmother was the only person she had left, and that they had to sleep and live under such terrible circumstances. Betsy decided to do something about it by sponsoring her.

A World Vision worker was able to visit Maggie last year and discovered a beautiful, happy young girl who was living with her great-grandmother in a new home. What did Maggie say about the difference this made in her life?

A lot of things have changed. The big difference is my house. We used to get soaked when the rains came. Now we're dry," Maggie said. *"We are able to eat three meals in a day. I started going to school, and I'm so determined! I* am able to answer questions when the teacher asks. As I get educated, I will be able to look after my grandmother.

Maggie's great-grandmother told the World Vision worker, "You used to come sit with us and get soaked by the rain. You used to say God will provide everything. Now all is well."

Perhaps the most amazing thing of all is that Maggie's hollow, empty eyes have been replaced by a sparkle and a hope for the future. Maggie wants to become a manager with World Vision. By sponsoring Maggie, Betsy didn't change the whole world, but she changed the world for one little girl. God can now use that little girl to make a difference for others.

Maggie

This is part of the miracle of taking your best shot and doing something bigger than yourself. Miracles like this are happening every day, everywhere, and anywhere one person decides to make a difference.

God is doing the impossible. Isn't it time, then, to begin to dream again of things that only he can do? Isn't it time to believe like we did when we were nine years old, when the sky was the limit? We have the opportunity and the responsibility to make a difference, whether that means changing the whole world or changing the world for one person.

God wants to use you.

The time is now.

Life is short and the world is waiting.

It's time to do something bigger than yourself.

Are you ready to take your best shot?

"When did we ever see you sick or in prison and visit you?"

And the King will say, "I tell you the truth, when you did it to one of the least of these my brothers and sisters, you were doing it to me!"

—Matthew 25:39-40

Acknowledgments

There are so many people involved in Hoops of Hope, it's hard to say thank you without missing someone. Before I begin, though, I'd like to say thank you to God. It was God who laid this on my heart and brought people around me to support my passion. There is no question about it; all the glory for anything any of us have ever done or will do, goes to the Creator of all who has a plan for each of us, loves us immensely, and wants a relationship with us. Thank you, God, for using me.

I'd also like to thank:

My mom and dad for always encouraging my heart and passion.

My grandparents and friends who were there encouraging me from the first shot.

The entire World Vision staff for inspiring all of us to do more, to give more.

Dana Buck for saying yes to a nine-year-old.

My school, Gilbert Christian School, and church,

Central Christian of the East Valley, for opening your hearts and facilities to kids—you never said no.

All the donors who have ever given, whether you gave one dollar or ten thousand, you have forever changed the lives of children a world away.

All the participants who worked tirelessly to shoot free throws for children they may never meet.

All the volunteers who have assembled and moved more hoops than imaginable.

The entire team at Thomas Nelson and Alive—thank you all for making the dream of a book a reality. Specifically:

Joel Kneedler, my literary agent. Thank you for believing in the Hoops of Hope story, guiding us with your professional knowledge, and pursuing the best co-author and publisher.

Todd Hillard, for patiently listening and working with me to tell the story. You were able to capture the true essence of the story and helped to tell it in an incredible way. I can't thank you enough.

MacKenzie Howard, our tireless editor. Your dedication and passion to the project were way over the top. Thank you for the long days and late nights you devoted to ensure the book would be its very best.

Joel, Todd, and MacKenzie, I believe God perfectly fit all four of us together to create an amazing team.

The Revolve Tour for allowing me to share each week and for setting the example of what you want my generation to be—World Changers!

The media, especially John Yeager of World Vision. Thank you for relentlessly telling the Hoops of Hope story—awareness is everything. And you still owe me a bungee jump over the Zambezi! I'd also like to thank Lisa Berglund, John Larson of NBC, Davy Finch, and Pete Radovich of CBS for traveling to the beautiful country of Zambia to help tell the story. Your coverage has helped spread the message, and now thousands of children have the access to the education and health care they need to survive.

And finally, to all the people and the children of Africa. Thank you for telling your stories. Your stories have changed us and forever will. All of us have so much to learn from you.

Ministry Resource Guide

Are you interested in going on a short-term mission trip?
Youth for Christ Project Serve: www.yfc.org/projectserve/
Youth with a Mission: www.ywam.org
Student Venture: www.studentventure.com
Royal Servants: www.royalservants.org

Are you looking for something to be involved in year round? There are lots of needs and some tremendous opportunities to serve in our own backyards.

Invisible Children: www.invisiblechildren.com
International Justice Mission: www.ijm.org
The Salvation Army: www.salvationarmyusa.org

And remember your school! You can make an eternal difference right where you are.

Young Life: www.younglife.org
Fellowship of Christian Athletes: www.fca.org

Sponsorship

World Vision
There is nothing quite like sponsoring a child through World Vision. You've heard all about it in this book; now's the time to get alone with God and see if this is where he wants to use you to change the world for one. Go to www.hoopsofhope.org and click on the World Vision link to browse through the kids' pictures for yourselves. There's bound to be a new friend out there who needs your help and is waiting to change your life too.

Whatever your passions are, there's a ministry or an organization that matches it. And if not, start one! Go ahead. *Take Your Best Shot!*

And finally, keep in touch with us at Hoops of Hope. It's been a crazy ride so far, and we have no idea where God might be taking us in the future. But who knows? Maybe we will see each other on the free-throw line someday, or maybe our paths will cross at the end of some dusty road, deep in the heart of Africa.

www.hoopsofhope.org

Notes

1. "Maggie's Story," World Vision: Tom Costanza, Kim Riemland. DVD, 2004.

2. Ron and Charity Luce. *Re-Create Your World: Find Your Voice, Shape the Culture, Change the World.* (Ventura, CA: Regal Books, 2008).

3. Adapted from "Seven Wonders of the World" MotivateUs.com. http://www.motivateus.com/stories/7wonders.htm.

4. Tim Hansel, *Holy Sweat* (Dallas: W Publishing, 1987).

5. U.S. Department of State. "Trafficking Persons Report 2005." http://www.state.gov/g/tip/rls/tiprpt/2008/.

6. King5.com Local News. "Marysville Starbucks 'Pay It Forward' Chain Ends," http://www.king5.com/localnews/stories/NW_122107WAB_starbucks_pay_it_forward_KS.3ae18b27.html. February 2009.

About the Authors

Austin Gutwein: Because this remarkable young man decided to take action, thousands of children left behind by the AIDS epidemic now have access to food, clothing, shelter, a new school, and, finally, a medical testing facility. His story has been seen nationally on CBS Sports before the 2008 NCAA Final Four tip-off, and has been featured on the *Today Show*. As a speaker on the Revolve Tour, Austin reaches about 125,000 teenagers each year. He lives with his family in Phoenix, Arizona.

Todd Hillard is a freelance writer and is passionate about taking the dreams and stories of others and bringing them to life on the written page. He has seventeen years of pastoral experience and has written more than twelve books.

NOW AVAILABLE
FROM YOUR FAVORITE REVOLVE AUTHORS

Every girl's favorite spy into the world of boys — Chad has a knack for helping teenagers figure each other out. His new book, *Guys Are Waffles, Girls Are Spaghetti* breaks down the differences in the sexes in a humorous but honest way. Based on the best-selling book for adults by Bill and Pam Farrel, this book for teens helps guys and girls value their differences so they can build healthy relationships with the "alien gender."

A Revolve conference regular, Jenna teamed up with her dad, Max Lucado, to write her first book, *Redefining Beautiful* — a fresh perspective for girls on what they need to live a life of peace, joy, and confidence. Jenna invites girls to clear their closets of all the accessories they think are essential and replace them with the only thing that will truly give them the security they are looking for: God's love.

Inspired by the needs of kids half way around the world, nine-year-old Austin started the organization Hoops for Hope which uses basketball shoot-a-thons to raise money for orphans in Zambia. Now a teenager, Austin is inspiring other kids to take action and make a difference in his new book *Take Your Best Shot*. The book includes tons of ideas for ways kids of any age can get involved in their community and the world!

WWW.THOMASNELSON.COM

You might think you are **just one person** in this world, but to one person **you might be the world**.

To one person you could mean the chance for **clean water, nutrition, health care, spiritual growth** and an **education**.

To one person **you could mean the difference** between life and death.

To one person you could mean hope.